The Prince of Preachers

The Prince of Preachers

Charles Spurgeon

Christian Timothy George

CF4•K

Copyright © 2006 Christian Timothy George
Paperback ISBN: 978-1-78191-528-8
epub ISBN: 978-1-84550-873-9
mobi ISBN: 978-1-84550-874-6

First published in 2006 and reprinted in 2009 and 2024
ISBN: 978-1-84550-155-6

Published by Christian Focus Publications, Geanies House,
Fearn, Tain, Ross-shire, IV20 1TW, Scotland, U.K.
Tel: +44 (0)1862 871011; Fax: +44 (0)1862 871699
www.christianfocus.com; email:
info@christianfocus.com
Cover Illustration by Brent Donoho
Cover design by Daniel van Straaten
Printed and bound in Denmark by Nørhaven

Scripture quotations, unless otherwise stated, are taken from the King James Version (KJV) of the Bible.

Scripture quotations marked (NIV) are taken from the HOLY BIBLE, NEW INTERNATIONAL VERSION®. NIV®. Copyright©1973, 1978, 1984 by International Bible Society. Used by permission of Zondervan. All rights reserved.

All rights reserved. No part of this publication may be reproduced, stored in a retrieval system, or transmitted, in any form, by any means, electronic, mechanical, photocopying, recording or otherwise without the prior permission of the publisher or a licence permitting restricted copying. In the U.K. such licences are issued by the Copyright Licensing Agency, 4 Battlebridge Lane, London, SE1 2HX www.cla.co.uk

This book is based on the life of Charles Haddon Spurgeon. References to Queen Victoria are fictionalised, but largely based on anecdotal evidence, which may or may not be true. Other characters in the book are either true to life, or compilations of various people Spurgeon met with, and was influenced by, throughout his life: e.g. Henry, Mary, Edward and Francis. From educated people to house maids and beggar boys, Spurgeon, the Prince of Preachers, reached out to them with the message of the gospel of Jesus Christ, the King of Kings. We hope that this book will encourage you to find out more about Spurgeon, for yourself and his Lord and Master.

For Rebecca,

my best friend, loving wife,

and greatest fan – a woman of whom

this world is unworthy.

Contents

Introduction 9
The Queen of England in Disguise 11
A Burning Sermon on a Snowy Sunday 17
Preaching to the Poor 27
A Pilgrim's Progress 45
Oh, Susannah! 61
A Broken Balcony 75
Father to the Orphans 87
Memories from Mentone 105
Grace for Gout 119
The Queen Arrives 133
Author's Note 145
Charles Spurgeon: Timeline 146
Charles Spurgeon: Life Summary 148
Thinking Further Topics 149

Introduction

It takes only a spark to ignite a country. Charles Haddon Spurgeon was that spark. His preaching set hearts on fire, churches on fire, and all of England on fire! The ends of the earth felt the force of his influence. Australia, Africa, Jamaica, and New Zealand received his weekly sermons. By the year of his death in 1892, he had preached to millions of people and had baptized thousands.

Before the days of microphones and amplifiers, his voice reached those seated in the far back of the auditorium. The God who opened Spurgeon's mind to the Bible, and his ears to the truth, opened his vocal chords to the world. The small child sitting on the front row understood his every word. The elderly couple sitting in the distant balcony heard him too. He preached to the masses, and he preached to each listening individual. He preached to royalty, and he preached to orphans. He preached to minds, and he preached to hearts. History will forever know Charles Haddon Spurgeon as the Prince of Preachers.

The Queen of England in Disguise

Imagine you are in Kensington Palace, London, England.

The monarch of the realm, Queen Victoria, sighs as she stares through the frosted glass of the palace window. Closing her eyes, she touches the window to feel the fury of the winter weather. A shiver runs down her spine. Snowflakes dance outside, following the wild movement of the wind. She dreams of dancing too, dancing outside in the snow, to the rhythm of the icy air.

'Kensington Palace has been my home for fifty years,' she says, looking at Alice, her lady-in-waiting, standing across the bedroom. Alice was young and beautiful, reminding the Queen of her earlier years, of days long gone by.

'I have ruled my country, I have married and buried my husband, and I have neglected my own dreams for so long. Though I have eaten the finest foods,' Victoria continues, 'dined with the best people, and worn the richest clothes, life has become too predictable for me.' Wind whistles through the crevices of the palace. Victoria opens the window, welcoming the frozen breeze.

'Your Majesty!' exclaims Alice, running to the latch. 'It's a blizzard out there! You'll freeze to death!' She tightly closes the window and locks it. 'This is one of the coldest mornings in London; we wouldn't want you to get sick right before your appointment with the Prime Minister.'

Victoria walks away from the window, savouring the small amount of cold air that came in. She sits in a chair facing the red embers in the fireplace.

'Every morning is the same,' she says. 'I wake up, get dressed, and perform the routine duties of my royal position.'

Her lady-in-waiting adds another log to the fire.

'Yes, your Majesty,' she replies.

'When do queens have fun?' the monarch asks herself curiously as she watches sparks escape up the chimney. An idea formulates in her mind. 'Today will be different,' she whispers. More sparks fly into the air. 'Today will be dangerous,' she says. A smile appears on her face. 'Today will be an adventure!' Jumping to her feet, Queen Victoria exclaims, 'We don't have much time! We must be on our way! I have a surprise planned for us today.'

'But your Majesty, what about your schedule?' replies Alice, 'and the Prime Minister?'

'Cancel my schedule!' commands the Queen. 'Cancel all my appointments for the day! There is someone else we must see.'

'Someone else, Your Majesty? Who? Who could be so important?'

Ignoring her, Queen Victoria marches over to the window and reopens it. Fresh air invades the cosy room.

'I am the Queen,' she exclaims. 'And today will be different!' Wind swirls through the curtains. Shocked, Alice nods and lowers her head.

'Gather up the fireplace ashes!' demands the Queen.

'What? Why do you want to –.'

'Do it!' she exclaims, pointing to the fire.

'As you wish,' squeals the lady-in-waiting, running to the fireplace. Victoria stands in front of the mirror. Important documents fly from the desk onto the floor.

'I can't believe I am about to do this,' she mumbles under her breath. 'I've never done anything like this before. Queens don't do this kind of thing. What would people say if they knew I was going to –'

'Your ashes, your Majesty!' says Alice, trying to catch her breath. She places a bucket of ashes before the Queen, and curtsies.

A strange look appears on Victoria's face. It is a look that longs for freedom – a look that longs to escape this luxurious life. She knows she'll have to pay a price for her actions, but she figures it's worth it.

'You are not to speak to anyone about this!' she exclaims, as she grinds a handful of ashes between her palms and applies them to her eyebrows and cheekbones.

Amazingly enough, just a little black ash soon makes her face unrecognizable.

'Excellent!' exclaims the Queen, as she examines herself in the mirror.

'Has she gone mad? Has she lost her mind completely?' Alice ponders. 'What if people find out about this?'

'Fetch me an old cloak from the servants' quarters!' demands the Queen, pointing to the door.

'As you wish, your Majesty,' replies Alice, scurrying out of the room.

Victoria's eyes dart wildly across the room.

'Freedom will soon be mine,' she whispers.

'Here it is,' announces the lady-in-waiting, entering the bedroom with a grey, musty cloak in her hand. Victoria goes to her mahogany writing desk and opens a drawer. She finds a sharp knife, a gold one she often uses to open her letters, and removes it from the drawer.

'This will do,' murmurs the Queen, a smirk on her face, as she walks towards Alice suspiciously.

Alice's eyes open wide as the Queen slashes the old cloak with the letter opener.

'I can't go outside looking like a queen,' Victoria tells her. 'It would be far too dangerous!' She puts on the torn cloak and walks to the window. A blanket of white snow covers the landscape.

'Follow me!' says the Queen, hurrying to the door. Her lady-in-waiting watches her. Dressed in the clothes of the poorest commoner, the Queen opens the bedroom door. Alice follows.

'What has come over the Queen?' she thinks, as she walks though the door frame. 'Why would she dress in the clothes of a peasant? Who is she going to see today? Who could be this important?' A gust of wind closes the door behind her, and the two women sneak out of the palace without being seen.

Who would have thought that the monarch and her lady-in-waiting were going to church ... to hear a preacher ... the Prince of Preachers himself? The lady-in-waiting didn't realise that, but the Queen was looking forward to it ... looking forward to it very much indeed.

A Burning Sermon on a Snowy Sunday

Colchester, England – the winter of 1849

It is Sunday morning, and it is hard to get out of bed! The wind whistles through the streets of Colchester, England, sprinkling flakes of snow upon the ground. The warm glow of the fireplace, and the hot sweet tea on the hearth, keep people inside, tucked away from the icy weather.

Charles, aged fifteen, loves hot sweet tea. It's his favourite drink. He places the cup to his lips and the soothing liquid warms his tongue, mouth, and throat. It travels deeper. But the heart of Charles Haddon Spurgeon burns already with a fire much warmer than hot tea. A burning question blazes through his mind: 'What must I do to be saved?' He cannot ignore the question.

He glances out the foggy window and sees a white snowy blanket stretch across the street. It is cold out there, but Charles burns to find an answer to his question. Putting down his cup of hot tea, he heads to the door. The leather boots slide on his feet, and the thick wool coat scratches his neck as he forces his arms through the sleeves. He hates cold weather! He loves sunshine. He loves the summer, when the warm air flows across the grassy fields, when he feels no care in the world, when he worries only about how much fun to have. He loves those happy times, but it is not summer, nor is it warm. A gust of icy rain smacks him in the face as he opens the wooden door to the outside blizzard.

As he walks, snow melts and trickles down the inside of his right boot. His sock soaks with water! Charles hates cold, wet socks. Now his whole body will shake and ache! A chill runs up his spine, as his foot slips into a puddle of slushy water. Too many times in his life he has stepped into puddles—puddles of cold water and puddles of problems. Too many times he has disobeyed his parents. Too many times he has chosen to do the wrong thing, instead of the right thing. Now his heart is heavy and his feet are cold.

Every snowflake that falls, reminds him of the sins that collect on the floor of his soul. He tries to be nice, but sometimes he's mean. He tries to tell the truth, but somehow ends up lying. He tries not to steal, but sometimes steals anyway. He often feels like a prisoner, unable to escape the terrible things he doesn't want to do. Like the apostle Paul, he continues to do the things he hates. A shiver of guilt grips him, as he yearns for forgiveness for his faults. He trudges through the snow and rain.

To Charles, church seems boring! It feels dry! Nothing really touches his heart in church. Nothing ever pricks his soul during the service. Growing up, he listened to many sermons, but none of them told him how to stop that dreadful sting of guilt. Like most of his friends, he considers church a place to sleep. But today, on this snowy Sunday, Charles wants to give church one more chance. He needs a place of answers, and he will combat a snowstorm to find them.

Born on 19th June, 1834, in the small village of Kelvedon, England, Charles learned of the storms his ancestors faced. One of his relatives, Job Spurgeon, refused to believe one of the wrong teachings of the church. He believed his Bible instead and was thrown in jail. During the bitter winter of that year, Job slept on hay and almost froze to death for his convictions. Charles walks and thinks of Job. His toes are almost completely numb. 'If my ancestors could deal with the cold,' he thinks, 'so can I.' His hope rises as he continues to crunch through the snow.

Storm clouds swirl above his head. Charles has walked for miles. Looking up, he knows he needs to get inside quickly before the storm comes. Squinting at the street sign, a rush of panic seizes him. He is lost! He glances around. Nothing looks familiar. Fear runs through his body.

'Where am I?' Charles asks himself. No one is in sight. The blizzard grows worse by the second.

His teeth chatter. He can no longer feel his feet! His coat no longer shelters him from the cold. His boots are full of ice water. Stumbling down a strange path, Charles grasps for something to hold onto. The wind screams. His eyes burn and he closes them. Hands outstretched, he longs for something to catch his fall.

'Oh God, if you're really there, help me!' Charles prays, as he wanders aimlessly through the snow. He remembers those warm, long ago days ... he is a child once more and he is sitting on his grandfather's knee.

Five-year-old Charles Spurgeon has been allowed to stay up past his bedtime. Storytelling is a tradition Charles loves more than anything. The scarier the story, the more he likes it. Grandfather is in the mood to tell the young boy a story. 'There is a pit, young man, a bottomless pit,' his grandfather tells him during story time. Charles' eyes grow wide and interested.

'It is a very dangerous pit! The poor souls who fall into it never reach the bottom.'

'They fall forever?' Charles asks, bewildered.

'Forever and ever!' replies his grandfather. 'In fact, I can almost hear one falling soul look to another and ask, "Are you near the bottom yet?" "No," the other one replies, "I've been falling for a million years and will always fall, for this is the bottomless pit."'

'Who falls in the pit?' Charles asks.

'Those who do not know God will fall there when they die. Those who did not trust Him, or love Him, or serve Him when they were alive, fall away from Him forever when they meet their moment of death.'

'I hate heights! I don't want to fall!' Charles screams.

'And so you won't, young man. God has great plans for you. The Lord will bring you to love Him, and He will make you a fine preacher of His Holy Word. You will be used to save many souls for the Kingdom, and lives will be changed through God's power in you.'

That night, five-year-old Charles lies awake in his bed, his eyes wide open. A cold sweat covers his face. He doesn't want to die without God. He doesn't want to be separated from Him forever. As the lids of his eyes grow heavy, he begins to wonder if God will save him when he dies. His room grows darker and darker. Charles doesn't want to close his eyes. What if he never opens them again? He doesn't want to fall forever in that deep, dark pit.

'God, please help me,' young Charles whispers. 'I don't want to die without you in my life.'

In the middle of his memories, Charles stumbles and falls in a faint, thrusting out his arms to protect himself in the blizzard. His arms come up against something. A door? A gate? Loud singing wakes him from his stupor and he rubs his eyes. An open church door comes into view and Charles can hardly believe that he has found what he was looking for all along. His head throbs as music fills his ringing ears. Still dazed and dizzy, he stands to his feet. He has fallen into a church!

'Where am I?' Charles asks. He walks around the corner and sees a sanctuary with an enormous, wooden pulpit in the front. Everything smells old and musty. This is quite a different church than the one he intended to find this morning, but nonetheless, it is still a church.

'Maybe I can find my answer here?' he wonders. He takes off his coat and sits on a back pew. Only fifteen people sit around him. Charles tries to remain unseen, but he can't. He wants to be invisible, but he knows he looks like a wet rat! Everyone looks at him.

Charles tries to sing with the congregation, but their singing is so loud that he can barely hear himself think. He has never heard such a small crowd make such a big noise. Eventually, the singing stops and Charles breathes a sigh of relief. His ears ring from the noise. Oddly, minutes pass by in silence, and no one goes to the pulpit to preach.

'This is hopeless,' Charles thinks. 'I came all this way and there is not even a preacher to tell me how I might be saved!'

An old, thin, shoemaker sees that the pastor is not in the church. Assuming the pastor is probably snowed up somewhere on the road, the shoemaker stands to his feet and heads to the pulpit. Charles grows curious.

'Let us look in the book of Isaiah,' the shoemaker says, 'to hear the Word of the Lord!'

Everyone opens a Bible.

Charles chuckles to himself as he watches the old, uneducated shoemaker attempt to preach in the pastor's place.

'Is this a joke?' he thinks. 'He can't even pronounce the words correctly!' Putting on his coat, Charles stands up to walk back home.

'Look unto me, and be ye saved, all the ends of the earth!' the shoemaker exclaims, quoting from Isaiah.

Charles freezes in his steps. 'What did he just say?'

'Young man!' the shoemaker yells. Charles turns around and sees the old man pointing at him!

'This has never happened in church before,' Charles thinks.

'Young man, you look quite miserable!' continues the preacher.

Charles knew this was true, but he was not used to being told so. Shocked and confused, Charles sits back down in his seat.

'And you will always be miserable unless you obey my text!' yells the shoemaker.

Charles wonders, 'How did that preacher know I felt miserable?' The wind slams against the windows and tries to drown out the preacher's words.

'Now, looking doesn't take a great deal of pain!' says the shoemaker. 'It ain't lifting your finger or your foot; it is just, look. A man needn't go to college to learn to look! You may be the biggest fool in the world, but you can look! Anyone can look; even a little child can look!'

Hope fills Charles' heart. The storm violently surges, but the soothing words of the shoemaker continue.

'Many of ye are looking to yourselves, but it's no use looking there! You'll never find any comfort looking to yourselves. Look unto Jesus and be saved! Jesus says to you this morning, "Look unto me; I am sweating great drops of blood. Look unto me; I am hanging on the cross. Look unto me; I am dead and buried. Look unto me; I rise again. Look unto me; I ascend to heaven. Look unto me; I am sitting at the Father's right hand. O poor sinner, look unto me! Look unto me!"'

For the first time in his life Charles looks. *Look unto me and be ye saved!* He looks, and he looks, until he almost looks his eyes away! Suddenly, the storm outside is silent. No longer can its wind and rain keep him from the truth. Charles looks to God and feels God looking back. Warm sunlight pours through the colourful church windows. The black clouds roll away. Finally, the truth of God and the power of the Holy Spirit enter the heart and mind of young Charles Haddon Spurgeon.

For the first time, everything is clear. Everything is bright. Everything makes sense. His dirty sins are washed away, and Charles gives his life to Jesus. God fills him with a fresh peace. A smile spreads across his face.

As the service concludes, Charles steps outside. The sun has started to melt the snow, and the black clouds have blown away. The air seems clearer than before. And his heart – the heart God set on fire early that morning – the heart God brought to church to hear a burning sermon on a snowy Sunday – the heart that was restless for so long – finally grows calm as it finds its rest in the Lord.

Preaching to the Poor

Cambridge, England – Sunday afternoon, 1851
It was a hot summer day – just the way Charles liked it. Sixteen-year-old Charles lay on his back in the middle of a field, soaking up all the sunshine he could. The cold months of winter were gone, along with his bitter feelings of shame, guilt, and despair. A new light was shining in his life. His relationship with Jesus grew stronger every day. The tall Cambridge grass rolled like waves across a grainy sea. Time forgot to tick.

'I love it here,' Charles said to Henry, his new friend and fellow classmate. Henry was tall and had brown, curly hair. All the girls liked him. He was quite the opposite of Charles. He was the best cricket player at school, and his well developed frame reflected it.

Henry pointed in the air. 'Charles, what do you see when you look at that cloud?'

Charles studied it for a moment. 'It looks like a cross,' he said. He turned his head sideways to get a better view.

'A cross?' Henry said. 'How can you look at that cloud and see a cross? It clearly looks like a hammer – the kind judges use in courtrooms.'

Henry grabbed a handful of grass and threw it at Charles' face. Charles attempted to roll out of the way, but he was too slow and much too plump to avoid such an assault. The dry clump of wheat exploded upon impact and fell down his shirt.

'You're going to pay for that!' Charles kidded him, lunging in his direction. 'I might not be as quick or athletic as Henry,' Charles thought, 'but if I can pounce on him, the war will be won!'

Henry tried to run away, but he was laughing too hard. Charles succeeded in his strategy, and Henry landed on the ground with a loud THUD! Henry wasn't worried – he knew Charles' weakness, and he fought back with handfuls of grass. Charles quickly gave up, unable to tolerate the dirty grass being forced into his mouth.

Henry looked back up at the cloud. 'Charles, do you really see a cross up there?'

Charles spat out the grass and nodded.

'That's what I like about you,' Henry said, dusting off his hands. 'You see God in everything!'

Charles was trying to remove a piece of grass that was lodged between his upper teeth. 'Last winter,' he said between spits, 'God changed my life. Ever since that snowy morning in Colchester, nothing has been the same.'

Henry pointed to a tree growing on the edge of the field. 'Let me ask you a question, Charles,' he said. 'What word comes to mind when you look at that tree?'

Charles looked at its leaves, its thick, brown trunk. His eyes followed its wood, all the way down to the well-developed root system, nourishing it. 'Grace,' Charles said.

'Grace? What do you mean?'

Charles pointed to the river running by the tree. 'Well, that tree depends on the river for vitality. God could have planted it somewhere else – by a forest or on a mountain. But if He had, this tree's roots would not be as strong or its trunk as broad. Grace gives that tree its green leaves.'

Henry was amazed. Charles' logic made good sense to him. 'When you were young,' he said, 'what did you think of church?'

'Oh, I hated to go,' Charles said. 'It was such a bore!'

Henry snapped his fingers. 'And just like that – your attitude changed?'

Charles paused. 'When God changes us, for some, it happens early in life; for others, it happens later. In my case, God waited until last year to show me the truth. I learned that I really was a sinner. I really needed a Saviour. And ever since that moment in that chapel, when I surrendered my life to Him, the world has taken on new meaning for me.'

Henry could listen to Charles talk about God for hours. His language was simple, yet somehow profound. It came from the sincerest part of his soul. There was nothing artificial about his faith.

Charles continued. 'Henry, we are not wild trees, growing all by ourselves in the middle of a jungle. We did not plant ourselves, you know. God is the Great Gardener, planting us by streams of living water.'

'Why did God bring you here?' Henry asked. 'Why did God plant you in Cambridge?'

'My parents sent me here to get a better education,' Charles said, 'but I miss them already. It's been only one month since I left Colchester.'

'And why did you choose to join Saint Andrew's Baptist Church? There are other Baptist churches here in Cambridge – Eden Chapel and Zion Chapel. Why did you come to my church?'

Charles sat up. 'My first Sunday in Cambridge was difficult. I was in a new city. I didn't know anyone. I went to your church because it was near the centre of town, not too far away from where I live. No one spoke to me that first Sunday, but when I heard the preacher pray, I felt the Holy Spirit leading me to attend there regularly. By the second week, members from the congregation invited me to their houses. We had great conversations. We talked about God and how He has changed our lives. On my third Sunday in Cambridge, the pastor called me into his office and asked me if I wanted to teach a children's Sunday school class. I was overjoyed to accept the position.'

'I have seen how you prepare your lesson,' Henry said. 'You spend so much time reading, I really think you should be teaching the adult Sunday school class, not the children's.'

'I love talking to children about God,' Charles said. 'Their faith is so fresh!'

Henry agreed. 'I have only known you for a few weeks, but I have seen how you read your Bible. You soak the Scriptures up like a sponge. You discover large nuggets of truth in the shortest verses of the Bible. During the week, when everyone is playing ball outside or studying hard for their classes, I find you walking through fields, talking with God. I wish my faith was as strong as yours. Is it true what they say? Do you really stay awake all Saturday night, preparing for your lesson on Sunday?'

Charles laughed. 'I don't stay awake all night,' he said. 'Sunday morning is the highlight of my week. I love sharing the gospel with the children who attend the class, and the reason I stay up so late is because I want to be fully prepared to present the gospel in all its truth and tenderness to them. Unfortunately, I want to talk longer to them than time allows.'

Henry thought about his own relationship with Jesus. 'When God came into my life,' he said, 'it was the greatest thing that has ever happened to me! I was a mess before Jesus took hold of me. There were times when I deliberately disobeyed my parents and sneaked away to be with girls, one girl in particular.'

Charles thought about it. 'Henry, we're too young to get married. That's why marriage is usually arranged for us by our parents.'

Henry continued. 'When my parents found out, they forbade me ever to see her again. The more they discouraged my feelings for her, the more I struggled with the temptation. And then I met Jesus. It was the turning point of my life. At first it was difficult, but I learned to submit to my parents' wishes. I found that my parents didn't make rules to hurt me. They made them to help me. They were right all along.'

Charles thought about his limited experience with girls. He had never 'been in love' with a girl before and wondered what it would feel like. 'Do you think a day will ever come when boys and girls will decide for themselves who to marry?'

'Maybe one day,' Henry said, 'but probably not for a hundred years or so.'

The sky turned twilight. They had completely lost track of time.

'It's getting late,' Henry said. 'We'd best be on our way.'

Charles wanted to talk more about girls, but Henry stood to his feet. 'Where are we going?' Charles asked.

Henry looked puzzled. 'Didn't James tell you?'

'James who?'

'James Vinter. He is a member of our church and the Director of the Lay Preachers' Association. Every week he sends young preachers out into the community to share the good news of the gospel. Tonight, he wanted us to go to the village of Teversham.'

Charles didn't understand. 'I do remember someone talking with me about this, but I didn't think he was serious. I'm too young to help lead a worship service.'

Henry put his arm on Charles' shoulder. 'All we have to do is go to Teversham and fellowship with the people there. That shouldn't be too hard.'

Charles looked suspiciously at Henry. 'Is this another joke?' he asked, ready to pounce on him again.

'It's no joke, Charles. James must have seen something inside of you and thought you would do a good job.'

Charles waited for Henry to burst into laughter and tell him the truth. He kept waiting ...

'I'm serious,' Henry interrupted. 'They are depending on us tonight. Teversham is about four miles away. We need to be leaving now.'

Henry wasn't lying. 'I've never done this before,' Charles thought. 'What if something goes wrong?'

Henry saw the nervous look on Charles' face. 'I will be there with you,' he said. 'What's the worst that could possibly happen?'

Charles could think of a few things. 'Well, for one,' he said, 'they could laugh us all the way back to Cambridge for being so young.'

Henry shook his head. 'If God has selected us to go there, He will see us through.'

Charles agreed, but didn't want to. 'Since Henry will be preaching,' Charles thought, 'the least I can do is go with him and help lead the music or a prayer.'

Charles looked at Henry.

'If James Vinter wants us to go to Teversham tonight, I will joyfully accompany you.'

'That's the spirit!' Henry said, stretching for the journey.

Henry was taller than Charles and walked slightly faster because his legs were longer. Charles wanted to keep up, but couldn't.

'It's not fair, God,' Charles prayed. 'Why didn't you make me more athletic like Henry? Why do I have to suffer in this fat body?' Charles grew tired and started to sweat profusely. 'I wish I were different. I wish I were stronger.'

'Are you alright?' Henry asked, looking back at Charles.

'Oh, I'm fine,' Charles lied. 'I just wasn't expecting the long walk, that's all.'

In reality, he was exhausted and thought about his weight problem. There were times in his past when he felt so insecure, that he sank into depression. Sometimes he would lock himself in his room, refusing food and friends. He wished God would change his appearance.

Charles and Henry walked through the narrow streets of Cambridge. Charles loved everything about it—the cobblestone streets, the festive markets, and, of course, the beautiful gardens that reminded him of his grandparents' country home. Charles was often inspired to draw the lush Cambridge scenery. He had the eye of an artist. Every once in a while, when the afternoon heat grew unbearable, he would take pencil and paper and sketch the steeple of a church or the curve of a bridge while sitting underneath the shade of a tree.

Charles loved other things, too: astronomy, mathematics, Latin, history, and geography. Some of the greatest thinkers in the world lived and taught in Cambridge. Charles enjoyed the exposure to new ideas, and he thrived in this environment. Charles read about six books every week. This habit would continue throughout his life. Sometimes, Henry would tease him about it, but Charles didn't care. Opening the pages of a book was like raising the sail of a ship – the possibilities for adventure were endless. He read books about hunting, travelling, science, and sports. He wanted to know as much as possible about God's great earth. Books brought joy to his life. Ever since he was young, he surrounded himself with them. It was in a dusty attic that he stumbled across the first book he ever read, a book he would soon collect: *The Pilgrim's Progress.*

As they walked to Teversham, the moon glistened above the fields of Cambridge. Charles did not enjoy the scenery because his joints were too inflamed. His ankles burned with pain – throbbing, swelling, aching to no end. He had to stop. 'I hope Henry is as tired as I am.'

'I need to take a break,' Charles finally said.

'We can stop here for a second,' Henry said, sitting down on the side of the road. Charles fell to the ground in sweet relief. He removed his leather shoes and rubbed his red, swollen ankles.

'So, what are you going to preach on tonight?' Henry asked.

Charles was confused. 'What did you say?'

Henry repeated himself, only louder.

'Very funny,' Charles laughed. 'But as you can see from the blisters on my feet, I am not in the mood for jokes.'

'Who said I was joking?'

'Who said I was preaching?' Charles replied. 'You are the one who is going to preach, not me!'

'That's not what James told me. He said that you were going to preach, and my job was simply to give you support and encouragement. So, what are you preaching on?'

Charles gasped and panicked. 'I've never preached a sermon in my life! What on earth will I say?'

'Charles, you bleed the Bible. Just talk with them about your love for Jesus, like we did earlier. They'll listen.'

Charles could not think clearly. 'Has Mr. Vinter tricked me into preaching? If Henry knew all along, why didn't he tell me about it earlier? Why is this happening to me?'

Charles Spurgeon

Henry saw the confusion on Charles' face. 'Mr. Vinter must have known you would reject an invitation to preach. Perhaps this is God's way of stretching you.'

Charles was not happy about the situation. 'I can preach to children,' he supposed. 'They are younger than me. But how can I preach to those who are older and more experienced in the Christian faith? What could I tell them that they do not already know?'

'God will give you the words,' Henry said. 'Like that tree you told me about, God will give you the nourishment you need. I have a feeling you were destined to preach.'

Charles had heard those words before. 'My grandfather used to say that,' he said. 'I know God gives us words when we need them, but I want God to give them to me now.'

Henry helped Charles to his feet, and they continued on their journey.

'I really need you now, God,' Charles prayed. 'I have no clue what I am going to say.'

Teversham was the opposite of Cambridge. It was a small village. There were not too many scholars living in Teversham. Vast fields surrounded simple houses. It was a farming village – the kind that barely makes the map.

Henry pulled Mr. Vinter's hand-drawn map out of his pocket and tried to navigate. 'I wish you had drawn this, Charles,' he said. 'We would have been there by now. It looks to me, however, that we are going to be worshipping in a cottage tonight, not a church.'

'A cottage?' Charles asked. 'I've never worshipped in a cottage before. Will there be a pulpit to hide behind?'

'Probably not,' Henry smiled. 'And there might only be a handful of people there – just some local families in the area.'

Charles relaxed. 'Perhaps with God's help, I really can tell a few farmers about the sweetness and love of Jesus!'

Light shone through house windows as they walked through the town. 'I wish I had my drawing tools with me!' Charles said, wanting to capture the scene on paper.

'You have a wonderful gift for drawing, Charles,' he said. 'But tonight you must use your gifts to sketch on people, not on paper. Draw a portrait of Jesus on their hearts. Paint a picture of the gospel.'

A small house stood before them. 'There it is,' Henry said, pointing to the cottage. There were no stained-glass windows or steeples or anything 'churchy' about it. It was a simple little place with a thatched roof. A faded wooden fence surrounded its border. Several trees towered over the fence.

'Perhaps my grandfather's prophecy was true,' Charles thought. 'Perhaps I will become a preacher after all.'

Henry saw the twinkle in Charles' eye. 'Are you ready?' he asked.

'I was born ready,' Charles replied, feeling a mysterious peace sweep over him.

Knock. Knock. Knock. An elderly woman opened the door.

'Which one of you is our preacher?' she asked, looking the two boys up and down.

Henry pointed to Charles.

'I am the preacher for the evening, madam,' Charles confidently said.

'And how old are you, boy?'

Charles didn't hesitate in responding. 'I am under sixty.'

The woman erupted in laughter. 'And under sixteen, too!' she exclaimed.

Charles humoured her with a smile.

'Come this way,' she said. 'The service is about to begin.'

The house was decorated with all sorts of wooden furniture. It soothed Charles' nerves and brought him comfort.

'Henry, I was really nervous back there on the road,' Charles whispered.

'I know you were. I didn't think you were going to make it. I thought I was going to have to carry you here.'

'I can't explain it,' Charles said, 'but there's no place I'd rather be than right here, inside this cottage, about to preach my first sermon.'

Henry knew God was equipping Charles with the power of the Holy Spirit. Preaching was too important a task to be done without God's help.

'I want to tell you something, Charles,' Henry said, keeping his voice low enough that the elderly lady would not hear him.

'Can it wait until after the service?'

'No, Charles, you need to hear this right now. You are not as athletic as I am, nor nearly as handsome.'

Charles punched Henry playfully in the stomach. They both laughed.

'Seriously, Charles. I want you to know that God has made you just the way He wants you to be.'

'What are you trying to say?' Charles asked, defensively.

'You are that tree, Charles. You are planted by streams of living water! God has hand-selected you to be a preacher of His Word. God doesn't waste anything. If you have experienced something, God will somehow use it for His glory. God has given you so many experiences. Don't you see, Charles? You are going to preach the light of the gospel in this dark land.'

Charles listened to his words. They were comforting and encouraging.

'But to be honest,' Henry said jokingly, 'I'm just glad you are preaching and not me.'

Charles laughed as they entered a small kitchen. Nine farmers stood against the back wall. Four of them had brought their wives and children. The kitchen table had been removed to give Charles a place to preach. Except for a few cooking pots on the walls and some plates stacked on the counter, the room was relatively empty. Parallel planks lined the ceiling of the room, keeping the roof from collapsing. The woman took Charles by the arm and ushered him in front of the small congregation.

'Give us some good preaching, boy,' she said and handed him a well-worn Bible.

Charles loved old Bibles – the worn feel of them. The one he held in his hand was falling apart at the binding. He knew that a worn Bible usually reflected a strong faith. As he looked into the eyes of the farmers, a thought came to his mind: 'Maybe I really can preach to adults. In a way, everyone who believes in God is a child of God.'

Henry was right; God did give Him a special gift, and with the help of the Holy Spirit, Charles Haddon Spurgeon began to preach his first sermon.

'Listen to the words of the Bible,' he said, pointing to the words. 'God is precious to those who believe in Him' – that is my text for the evening.'

The farmers looked strangely at him. They were not accustomed to hearing such boldness come from the lips of a sixteen-year-old boy from the country. Charles spoke firmly, without fear of what others thought of him. They listened to his words and were amazed. His voice was young, but somehow very mature.

'God has always been precious to those who love Him,' Charles preached. 'Remember Daniel in the lions' den? God was precious to him when angels closed the mouths of the lions. Remember David, the shepherd boy? God was precious to him when he slaughtered great Goliath. Remember Jonah? God was precious to him when a whale saved him from the bowels of the ocean. God has been precious to His people throughout the ages. Is He precious to you this evening?'

Whispers filled the cottage. Everyone wanted to know who this young man was. He looked far too young to know so much about the Christian experience.

'Excuse me,' Charles said, over the sound of their voices. 'There will be no more whispers during the service.'

Children giggled in the corners of the kitchen as their parents were chided.

'Even for we who believe,' Charles continued, 'there are times when we treat God like He is not precious to us. We turn away from God and are disobedient. We break His laws every day. In fact, there are times when we treat Him worse than we treat our enemies.'

Henry was astounded. It was like Charles was stretching his God-given wings for the first time.

'In my own life,' Charles said, 'I have doubted God's sovereign plan. I have doubted that the Lord could use a bad person like me to accomplish His perfect plan. We are all like blank pieces of paper, I suppose – helpless and hopeless without the artistic touch of God. But when God takes His providential pencil to us, He makes us the masterpiece we will be. We are all inadequate and unworthy as we stand before the throne of God. But God loves us anyway. No matter how ugly we are, or how depressed we may become, in the hands of the Lord we are precious pearls. Have you ever felt like you were not worthy to be God's friend?'

Charles paused for the reply.

'Yes, preacher!' one of the farmers cried, breaking the silence. 'I have felt that way!' Others nodded in agreement.

'Well, I have come all the way from Cambridge to tell you that He has not forgotten you! He has not abandoned you! He has not left you to yourselves. He loves you, and He died for you. If you believe in Him with all your heart, you will be saved from your sins. God will become the most precious thing in your life.'

Charles preached on. Like a great artist adding the finishing touches to his canvas, Charles concluded his sermon with a touch of gold. 'If you believe in Jesus with all your heart, soul, mind, and strength, and you confess that you are a sinner in need of salvation, you will be saved. Look to the cross this evening, dear congregation. Look to the cross!'

The Prince of Preachers

Some sniffled. Others fought back tears. Everyone was struck with amazement at the young man's sermon. Never before had a preacher preached the gospel with such power in that cottage. They were accustomed to dry, stale sermons that were typical of the day. But this young man brought the Bible back to life for them. He had touched their hearts with the freshest message they had ever heard. After hearing Charles preach, every person in that kitchen felt a little closer to God.

After the sermon, Henry approached Charles. Charles was hoarse from the sermon, but his heart burned with vigour. 'You were right,' he whispered, 'God does give us words when we need them.'

After promising the farmers that they would return as soon as possible, Charles and Henry walked out of the cottage.

'You will make a fine preacher, young man,' the elderly woman said, patting Charles on the head. 'If you are this good at sixteen, I would love to hear you at sixty!'

Everyone waved goodbye as Henry and Charles disappeared down the street.

As they walked back to Cambridge on New Market Street, Henry walked at Charles' pace. 'God will do great things in your life, Mr. Spurgeon,' he said. 'This is only the beginning!'

A Pilgrim's Progress

Cambridge, England – 1852

The house was large – large enough to get lost in. It was the mansion of the great publisher, Mr. Daniel McMillan. Luxurious rooms stretched through the rich estate. Crystal chandeliers hung from ceilings. Even the gardens that grew behind the house were carefully groomed and spaciously situated between lovely pieces of architecture. This was no typical Cambridge cottage, but it was a perfect place for eighteen-year-old Charles to meet Dr. Joseph Angus – the man who would talk to him about going to college.

On the train, Dr. Angus checked his watch. The ride had not been pleasant, and his head ached. To make matters worse, a young boy was misbehaving in the seat next to him.

'Who are you?' the boy asked.

Dr. Angus forced a smile. 'My name is Dr. Angus.'

'That's a funny name,' the kid replied, repeating it several times. 'Why are you going to Cambridge?'

Dr. Angus sighed. 'Maybe if I answer his questions, he will leave me alone.' 'I have an important meeting today,' he said, visibly annoyed.

'With whom?'

Dr. Angus turned around and looked for the boy's parents. 'Perhaps they can relieve me of this inquisition.' They were nowhere to be found. Dr. Angus changed his strategy and decided to overwhelm the boy with information. 'If you must know, young lad, I am the principal of Stepney Baptist College and I am on my way to Cambridge to meet a young preacher named Charles Haddon Spurgeon. He is a famous evangelist in these parts of England. They call him 'the boy preacher of the fens.' His father wrote me a letter last week and asked me to convince him to go to my college. He is many years older than you, but I'm sure when he was your age, his manners far exceeded yours.'

The boy said nothing – too much information to process.

'It worked.' Dr. Angus closed his eyes for the remainder of the train ride.

Charles gasped at the sight of the mansion. 'I have never seen a house like this before,' he thought. A golden plate hung from the door. It was so polished Charles could see his reflection. An ornate **M** was engraved in the gold.

Charles approached the door. He knocked three times. He waited. He knocked again. No answer. 'Maybe God does not want me to go to college after all,' Charles thought. Another three knocks. Suddenly, the door swung open and a young girl appeared. She had bright red hair. Her skin was fair and freckled.

'Are you Mr. Spurgeon?' she asked.

'Yes, that's right.'

'My name is Mary. Please, come in.'

Charles followed Mary into the enormous mansion. Tall mirrors hung from the highly decorated walls. 'This is a palace,' he thought, unable to believe his eyes. He looked at the beautiful oil paintings scattered throughout the room. 'Or maybe a museum.'

Charles had to ask. 'How much did those cost?'

'Too much,' Mary replied. 'Mr. McMillan has one of the largest collections of Italian paintings in Cambridge. They are gorgeous to admire, but difficult to clean.'

'How long have you worked here?' Charles asked.

Mary counted the years on her hands. 'About ten ... I suppose,' she said. 'Mr. McMillan is an honour to work for. His publishing company is well known throughout all of England.'

Mary stopped in front of a large, wooden door. 'I will leave you in the library for now.'

When she opened the door, Charles was overwhelmed by the thousands of books lining the walls. Oak bookshelves furnished the room, along with iron busts of philosophers, thinkers, and theologians. For Charles, this was like stepping into a magical world. Nothing brought a smile to his face more quickly than a room full of books. He skimmed the shelves. Some books were red, others blue. Some were faded, others new. It didn't matter what colour, shape, or size, if it had pages, Charles loved it. Running his hands along the highly-polished shelves, Charles searched for a particular book. 'Here it is,' he said, pulling it off the wall. The book had never been opened.

'Which one is that?' Mary asked.

Charles opened the book at the title page. 'This is one of the greatest books ever written,' he said. 'It's called *The Pilgrim's Progress*. I have read it over a hundred times.'

'A hundred times?' Mary blurted. 'What's so good about it?'

Charles didn't know where to begin.

'Have you ever read it?'

Mary looked at the floor. 'I never learned to read,' she said. 'For most of my life I have worked for Mr. McMillan. I'm really good at what I do, but I never had the opportunity to go to school. I would be grateful if you would tell me what the book is about.'

Charles felt sorry for her. She looked embarrassed. He opened the front cover of the book. 'Mary, this book is about a man named Christian. One day, Christian wakes up and finds a heavy burden on his back. He tries to get it off, but it's impossible – the burden is too heavy.'

Mary was intrigued. 'It sounds interesting.'

'Christian sets out on a journey and meets a man named Evangelist. Evangelist tells Christian how to get rid of his burden and find the Celestial City. Along the way, Christian encounters some very interesting characters. Some of them are trustworthy, others intend to harm him.'

'What's your favourite chapter?' she asked.

That was a good question. Charles liked them all. 'If I had to pick only one, I suppose my favourite chapter is when Christian fights the fire-breathing dragon, Apollyon!'

'Does he get hurt?'

'Yes,' Charles said, 'but he is wearing the armour of salvation.'

Charles saw Mary's enthusiasm.

'Does Christian ever lose the burden on his back?' she asked.

Charles smiled. 'Indeed, he does. One day, Christian is walking on the straight and narrow road and he sees a cross sitting on a hill. He runs to it, kneels before it, and in an instant, the burden falls from his shoulders and rolls into a tomb.'

'It just falls off?' she asked.

Charles snapped his fingers. 'Just like that. Christian jumps up and down because he is so happy.'

Charles sensed that Mary was bothered. 'What kind of burdens do you carry?' he asked.

Mary paused. 'I just want to fit in. Some people make fun of me because I can't read. I just want the laughter to stop. I live with my family about six miles (ten kilometres) from here, and each morning when I come to work for Mr. McMillan, I try to forget about my troubles. I busy myself to the point that I don't have time to be burdened. I really want to learn to read – it's frustrating having to clean this library every day and not being able to read its books.'

Charles put *The Pilgrim's Progress* on the desk. He walked to where she was standing. 'Mary, I want you to know something. Jesus loves you and He is the greatest teacher in the world. I have never been to college—some people ridicule me about that. But God teaches us everything we need to know for the season of life we are experiencing.'

Mary tried to conceal her emotions, but a tear escaped her eye. 'Mr. Spurgeon, some preachers say that Christians who don't read the Bible are disobedient. Five years ago, I stopped going to church altogether. I didn't think God could ever accept me the way I am.'

'Reading the Bible is important,' Charles said. 'It is one way God communicates with us. But there have been many Christians who never learned to read.' Charles had an idea. 'Mary, why don't you come to my church and we will teach you to read?'

'You have a church?' she asked, sniffing.

'Two years ago, I preached my first sermon in Teversham. Shortly after, a little church in Waterbeach called me to be their pastor. They are the warmest congregation and would love to get to know you.'

'How many people usually come?' she asked.

'When I first became their pastor, there were only fifteen people who regularly attended the morning service. God has now brought almost five hundred people to us.'

Mary raised her eyebrows. 'You must be a great preacher to attract all those people.'

'The gospel of Jesus Christ is what attracts people to our church – the simple story of God's great grace.'

'You seem very young to be a pastor,' Mary said.

Charles had heard those words a hundred times. 'Madam, you can never be too young to do the work of God.'

A distant voice called for Mary. 'I must go, Mr. Spurgeon. Mr. McMillan needs my assistance. But I have to ask you one more question before I go. How does *The Pilgrim's Progress* end?'

Charles smiled and reached into the pocket of his long coat to retrieve his own copy and handed it to her. 'I want you to discover the ending for yourself.'

Mary was so excited to learn to read, that she bumped into the desk on her way out. 'Thank you so much, Mr. Spurgeon! God bless you!' she said, smoothing her skirt.

Charles sat down in the library chair to pray. 'God, help Mary to learn to read, so she may discover the many blessings you have given us in your Holy Word.'

Charles thought about his own education – that was the reason he was at Mr. McMillan's house today. 'I never considered going to college before my father brought it up – he thinks I will be more prepared to do the work of the Lord with a theological degree. But Lord, you are my Heavenly Father. Is this also your desire for me?' Charles knew that going to college would force him to abandon his church at Waterbeach. He slumped in the chair, burdened by this important decision.

The train finally arrived at the station in Cambridge. Dr. Angus was eager to get away from the bothersome child. His head was throbbing harder now. He was not as young as he used to be. The journey and the constant chatter had made him grumpy and miserable.

Mumbling under his breath, he left the train station and entered a carriage. Handing Mr. McMillan's address to the driver he ordered, 'Take me here. And make it fast! I have an important meeting to make.' The carriage leaped into action, speeding off to the destination. The ride was bumpy, but Dr. Angus was just glad to be away from the child on the train. He checked his pocket watch.

It was approaching the time when he would meet with Charles. 'When I offer Charles the opportunity to study at my university,' he thought, 'I know he will agree. How could anyone turn down an opportunity like this?'

The carriage pulled into the estate, and Dr. Angus grabbed his leather briefcase. He shuffled through it, making sure all the papers Charles needed to sign were there.

'What's the hurry?' the carriage driver asked.

Dr. Angus didn't have time to explain. 'I am going to meet Mr. Charles Haddon Spurgeon today, sir, if you must know.'

'Mr. Spurgeon? The boy preacher?'

'He's the one.'

The carriage driver reached into his pocket and handed Dr. Angus a piece of paper.

'What's this?'

The driver smiled. 'I have heard great things about this young preacher. Would it trouble you to get his autograph for me?'

Dr. Angus shook his head. 'No, I am strictly here to convince him that he will be more useful to the Lord with a proper theological education.'

The carriage driver's face wrinkled. 'More useful to the Lord?' he asked. 'But he's already working so effectively for God.'

Dr. Angus was aggravated. 'You obviously do not know what God wants for him,' he told the driver. 'God wants him to be educated at my school!'

'You are entitled to your own opinion,' the driver said, 'but I think he should continue preaching in Waterbeach. So many souls are being saved.'

Dr. Angus handed the money to the driver. 'I am not paying you for your thoughts, dear sir, but I will offer you one of mine – perhaps you could use some education yourself!'

The Prince of Preachers

Dr. Angus stepped out of the carriage and walked up the stairs to the giant front door. The carriage quickly sped away. Briskly, he knocked on the door. A moment passed. He knocked once more. 'What is taking so long?' Dr. Angus wondered, impatiently. Just then the door swung opened.

'It's about time,' Dr. Angus complained, looking at the servant girl.

'Are you Mr. Angus?' she asked.

'My name is Dr. Angus,' he corrected. 'An educated girl would have known how to address her company.'

Mary was far from being educated and she hated to be reminded. 'Come right this way,' she said, noticeably hurt by his insensitive comment. Unaware that Dr. Angus was supposed to be meeting Charles, she led him down the hall, walked past the library, and showed him into the parlour.

'I hope you will be comfortable here,' she said.

'Comfort is a thing of the past,' he said.

Mary closed the door and left him by himself.

Charles browsed through the books until he grew tired. Two hours had passed since Mary had shown him into the library, and he was growing concerned. 'Where is Dr. Angus?' he wondered. 'Perhaps there has been a problem.' Charles thought. Every conceivable tragedy raced through his mind. 'Perhaps Dr. Angus did not think I really needed to go to college after all. Maybe his train was late. Maybe his carriage broke down on the side of the street.'

Charles rang the bell on the wall. Rrrrrring. 'Perhaps I was never meant to go to college after all,' he thought. 'Maybe this is God's way of keeping me at my church in Waterbeach.'

Mary promptly opened the door. 'Mr. Spurgeon, how can I assist you?'

'I am sorry to interrupt your work,' he said, 'but it has been two hours and my company has not yet arrived.'

Mary thought for a moment. 'Your company …' she said. 'I have not seen your company, but I did let a gentleman inside about an hour and a half ago. He was a very disgruntled man who complained about everything. I think his name was Dr. Angus.'

'Dr. Angus?' Charles asked. 'Oh no! He was my company. He was the man I was supposed to meet!'

'Dr. Angus was your company?' Mary asked, horrified by her mistake.

'Yes. Is he still here?'

'No, he waited an hour and then let himself out.'

Charles panicked. 'He probably assumed I did not want to meet him.'

'I am so sorry, Mr. Spurgeon. No one told me that you two were appointed to see one another. It's all my fault! Please forgive me! I am so sorry!'

Charles could not believe the situation. 'How could this happen? Dr. Angus travelled all the way from London to meet me.'

The Prince of Preachers

Mary began to cry, her freckled cheeks red with embarrassment. 'How could I have been so foolish?' she sobbed. 'How could I have let this happen?'

Charles pitied her, even though he was well aware of the implications of her mistake. 'Mary, do you believe everything happens for a reason?'

'I don't know,' she said. 'Maybe …'

Charles was not going to let this moment go by without talking about God's sovereign plan. 'I believe God controls everything,' he said. 'I cannot imagine worshipping a God who does not have a plan. Can you?'

Mary shrugged her shoulders. 'You think my mistake happened for a reason?'

'Precisely!' Charles exclaimed. 'God often uses our mistakes in mysterious ways.'

Mary looked up at Charles. 'I just ruined his day, perhaps his life's career. How can he be so sympathetic at such a time as this?'

'Do not think another thought about it,' Charles softly said. 'What's done is done.'

Mary wiped the tears from her eyes. 'Mr. Spurgeon, I am forever in your debt.' She showed him to the door.

Charles turned to leave. 'Oh, I almost forgot,' he said. 'Will we have the honour of seeing you at our church on Sunday?'

Mary had completely forgotten about the invitation. 'Why, of course,' she said, smiling. 'I wouldn't miss it for the world!' She watched Charles walk down the stairs and disappear. 'He really does have a pastor's heart,' she thought, closing the mansion door.

Charles began to pray, as was his custom when he walked. 'God, I want to be honest with you. I still feel frustrated about missing my appointment with Dr. Angus. Why did you let this happen to me?'

Charles passed Saint Andrew's Baptist Church, the church where he used to teach Sunday school. Someone was preaching in the sanctuary.

'How strange,' he thought, listening intently. 'It's not Sunday – why is someone preaching? Perhaps it is a Bible study or a lecture of some sort.' Charles walked in and sat down near the back.

'Do you seek great things for yourselves?' the preacher asked. A small congregation had gathered. Charles recognized neither the voice nor the man in the pulpit, but he felt compelled to hear him. He had learned long ago, not to walk out of a church service.

'Maybe some of you require big mansions or beautiful gardens to make you happy,' the preacher said. 'Others of you are only satisfied with worldly lusts and sinful vanities. Some might even be sitting here today thinking you need a better job or a fancier education so God can use you in His kingdom.'

Charles perked up.

'Well, let me tell you something, dear soul. Jesus does not want you to be confident in your own abilities. He wants you to be confident in Him. No matter what your occupation is, be content in it, for Jesus can satisfy your soul.'

'Well, I suppose that's true,' Charles thought.

'For the artist, God is altogether lovely. For the architect, He's the chief cornerstone. For the astronomer, He's the sun of righteousness. For the baker, He's the living bread. For the builder, He's the sure foundation. He's the door for the carpenter and He's the light of the world for the candle maker. He's the sower for the farmer, and for the florist, He's the lily of the valley. He's the precious living stone for the jeweller, and for the labourer, He's the giver of rest. Do you seek great things for yourself, dear friend?'

Charles pondered the question.

'Seek them not!' shouted the preacher. 'Seek them not!'

Charles stood up. He was so moved by the words of the preacher that he had to leave the sanctuary. He needed to talk with God, and he needed to do it quickly. Charles walked to the midsummer's common, a field where he often thought and prayed. He passed over the little bridge leading to Chesterton.

'Am I seeking great things for myself?' he wondered. 'Do I want to go to college for selfish purposes?'

Charles grew anxious and began to pray.

'Father, you have gifted me as a preacher. You have equipped me for that calling. Help me to surrender to your will. You know what is best for me. I will remain at the church you have given me in Waterbeach.'

Charles felt a flare of frustration, but knew that God wasn't in the business of making mistakes—he refused to worship a God who wasn't in control.

'Perhaps God led me to Mr. McMillan's house today so I could minister to Mary. She was very interested in *The Pilgrim's Progress*. Maybe it will draw her closer to God.'

Charles thought about Christian, the main character travelling to the Celestial City in *The Pilgrim's Progress*. 'Maybe being a pilgrim means that we have to learn to trust God more than we trust ourselves. Help me, Lord, to depend on your guidance, even when I do not know where my footprints will lead. Father, I don't need to know the future, but I need to trust that you are in it.'

Oh, Susannah!

*7 St. Ann's Terrace, Brixton Road, London,
England – 1856, 10 a.m.*

'So, is he handsome?'

'Well, he's a country boy,' Susannah told her aunt. 'He has dark, shabby, untrimmed hair, hazel eyes, and he's a bit overweight. His name is Charles Spurgeon.'

'A country boy?' her aunt replied. 'You were raised a city girl. I always thought you would marry a lawyer or a doctor or someone of equal stature.'

Susannah smiled and brushed a lock of chestnut hair behind her ear. 'He's smart enough to be a lawyer, and talented enough to be a doctor, but God called him to be a preacher, and he's a fine one at that! Auntie, he's not the tallest man on the planet – he gets his height from his short mother, but just wait until you hear him preach. He's the most charming man I've ever met.'

'He must be to capture your heart,' replied her aunt. 'You are one of the most beautiful girls in London. How did you meet him anyway?'

Susannah loved to tell the story. 'Charles was the pastor of a little church in Waterbeach. His church grew so rapidly, that London received news of it.

Our church, New Park Street, asked him to come to preach. Our attendance was going to be low that day and the only reason I went to hear his sermon, was because I felt sorry for him.'

Susannah poured some tea into a flowered cup and handed it to her aunt. Susannah loved tea. By nature she was very conversational and enjoyed nothing more than surrounding herself with friends, talking over a cup of hot, English tea.

'I'll never forget the first time I saw him,' she said. 'He looked terribly awkward. It was Sunday evening. Our church desperately needed supply preachers, but when I looked at Charles standing behind that pulpit, I knew we were scraping the bottom of the preacher bucket. Auntie, his clothes must have been cut by a blind tailor!'

'How so?' her aunt asked, smiling.

Susannah closed her eyes. 'Just imagine the sight – an ugly, black satin stock[1] hanging from his neck, dirty shoes that had never been cleaned. And his hair ... he looked like a peasant, not a preacher!'

Susannah's aunt erupted in laughter and had to place the cup of tea on the table for fear of spilling it. Susannah continued. 'Oh, but I have not even told you the worst of it ...' Her aunt braced for impact.

'Poking from his coat pocket was the most hideous blue handkerchief you have ever seen! It was covered with red polka dots. Every now and again, when

---

1. Leg-high socks worn by men during Victorian era.

Charles felt that he needed to make his point stronger, he would pull it out and wave it around like a flag! I have never seen anything so out of style in all my life! If the boy couldn't preach so well, I would have mistaken him for a monkey!'

Susannah's aunt shook with laughter, unable to contain herself. 'Sounds like he needs a woman's touch!'

Susannah liked the sound of that. 'After the wedding ceremony today,' she said, 'I am going to throw that hideous handkerchief into the wastebasket where it belongs.'

Many minutes later, after dozens of hilarious stories about Susannah's fiancé, they composed themselves.

Her aunt was curious. 'How did you fall in love with him?'

'It was gradual, I think,' Susannah replied. 'I knew there was something unique about Charles when I first saw him preach, but I never imagined that I would be walking down the aisle to meet him at the altar this afternoon. He preached for several months at our church and eventually became our pastor.'

'How old is he?' her aunt said.

'Twenty-two.'

Her aunt was astonished. 'He's so young to be a pastor.'

'That is the mysterious thing about him, Auntie,' Susannah said. 'He is young to be a pastor, but God has really anointed his ministry. He can preach to children and adults alike. He has such a way with words. Granted, he is rough around the edges, but when he steps into the pulpit, magic happens. His voice is melodic, penetrating, and pleasant. New Park Street Baptist Church has had some really great pastors in the past: Benjamin Keach, John Gill, and John Rippon, to name a few, but Charles is the best.'

Susannah's aunt was impressed. 'I can't wait to hear him preach! These days, preachers are so formal and rigid that they often forget about the people sitting in the pews. It will be good to hear a young, fresh voice opening the Word of God to people who need to hear it.'

'I know,' Susannah said. 'I've never heard someone explain the Bible so clearly. That's what makes Charles so interesting. He really connects with us. He enjoys taking short biblical texts – short phrases – and extracting great truths from them. If you give him an orange, he can squeeze a sunset out of it.'

'How did he acquire such ability?' asked her aunt.

Susannah didn't altogether know. That's what attracted her to him. 'When he lived in Cambridge, he taught a children's Sunday school class. I believe that might have contributed to the way he approaches the Bible. He uses common language – simple sentences with vivid word pictures. And yet, as the same time, he is never boring to listen to. He has read so widely that he draws analogies from every area of life. He can talk to anyone about anything! And his memory – flawless.'

'He doesn't use difficult vocabulary and complicated arguments?'

'Not at all,' Susannah replied. 'His language is earthy and real. Ever since I met him through a mutual friend in the church, I noticed how easily he addresses the deepest needs of the human heart. He is a man of answers. I began meeting with him to talk about some spiritual problems that were plaguing me. We were, of course, chaperoned.'

Her aunt was relieved. 'What kind of spiritual problems were you having, Susannah?'

'Before I met Charles, I went through seasons in my life where I doubted my salvation. How was I supposed to know if I was a Christian or not? I kept sinning and backsliding in my faith. But when I met Charles, everything changed. He opened my eyes to a truth I had never realized before – my questions alone were evidence that God was working in my life and wooing me with His love. And then he gave me this.'

Susannah pulled a wooden chest out from underneath the coffee table next to her chair. She raised its lid and pulled out a leather book. 'This book meant so much to him over the years. Other than the Bible itself, it is his favourite.' She handed it to her aunt.

'I recognize the title, *The Pilgrim's Progress*, but I have never read it,' her aunt confessed.

'It's about a pilgrim. Charles says we are all pilgrims on a journey. This book reflects our own pilgrimages. Charles has read it over a hundred times; he even collects them.'

'It looks very old,' her aunt said, trying not to crumble the binding.

'That was the first copy he ever owned. When he was living with his grandparents, he found it in their attic. I knew when he gave it to me that we would spend the rest of our lives together.'

Her aunt read the name of the author: 'John Bunyan ... who was he?'

'John Bunyan lived, about four hundred years ago, in Bedford. Like Charles, he was also a preacher. One day, while he was playing ball with his friends, Bunyan heard the voice of God ask, "Will you leave your sins and go to heaven, or have your sins and go to hell?" That question troubled him for many months, until at last it drove him to Christ's cross, and he found forgiveness for his sins. But this is where the story gets really interesting.'

The aunt listened attentively to her niece.

'In those days you needed a licence to preach, and since John Bunyan did not have one, he was thrown into prison. His wife and children depended on their father for financial support, so they suffered just as much as he did. But God had a plan for John Bunyan. Behind the bars of his cell, he wrote a story about the Christian life ... but he wrote it in the form of an allegory ... an adventure story with a double meaning. He named it *The Pilgrim's Progress*. It has become one of the world's greatest Christian stories.'

Her aunt read the words Charles had written for her in the front cover: 'Miss Thompson, with desires for her progress in the blessed pilgrimage. From C. H. Spurgeon, April 20, 1854.'

Susannah sipped her tea; it was slightly cold. 'And here we are, two years later, about to get married.'

'You must be the happiest girl in London,' her aunt said, smiling. 'At eight o'clock this morning, I passed the church on my way to your house. Hundreds of people were already standing outside, waiting to enter the sanctuary. A police division had to be called to control the crowds. Your marriage is the talk of the town.'

'Recently,' she said, 'Charles has been attracting some bad attention.'

'From whom?'

Susannah hated to think about it. 'Newspapers hate him, Auntie. They say all sorts of terrible things about his preaching and his character.' Susannah reached down and pulled several articles from the wooden chest. Look at this one – "Charles Spurgeon is a coarse, stupid, irrational bigot, a scavenger in the literary world – *The Saturday Review*."'

'How terrible!' her aunt said in disgust.

'Charles takes their words to heart and sinks into deep depression.'

'What degrees does he hold?' asked her aunt.

'Well, that's part of the problem,' Susannah said. 'Charles never went to university. Most preachers in London hold formal theological degrees, but Charles sticks out like a sore thumb. Of course, people don't realize that he taught himself Greek, Hebrew, and Latin when he was only a boy, and he has read far more books on theology than most preachers read in a lifetime. Personally, I think college would have been the worst thing in the world for him. Charles is too unique, too creative. His quick wit might have fizzled in an academic atmosphere. Who knows, he might have lost his respect for the Bible altogether by viewing it like any other textbook!'

It was time for Susannah's aunt to offer her some final words of womanly wisdom.

'Susannah,' she said, squeezing her hand. 'Listen to me carefully, my dear. There will be many difficulties in your marriage. God is entrusting you with the responsibility of loving Charles through thick and thin – when life is good and when life is troubling. From what you have told me, Charles is a great man, and great men get nowhere without great women in the shadows, praying for them and supporting them. You have finally found the man of your dreams. Never take him for granted, and I believe the two of you will live happily for ever.'

Susannah wrapped her arms around her aunt.

'On a lighter note,' remarked her aunt, 'we need to get you into your wedding dress!'

***

New Park Street Baptist Church, London, England – 12:00 noon

Never in its history had New Park Street Baptist Church looked so beautiful. Ribbons, candles, and the finest flowers embellished the auditorium. Charles' friends and family had arrived for the ceremony and they stood in the foyer outside the sanctuary. Charles stood at the front of the church, talking with Dr. Alexander Fletcher, the pastor of Finsbury Chapel and the man who would soon join them in marriage.

Charles' mother, Eliza, nudged her husband, John, in the ribs. 'We have brought seventeen children into this world,' she whispered. 'Look at him! Has he ever looked happier? He has one of the fastest growing ministries in this city, he is currently writing a book, *The Saint and His Saviour*, and he is marrying the most beautiful girl in all of London. What did we do to deserve such a wonderful blessing?'

John shook his head. 'And isn't it strange to think how Charles was born ten days after William Carey, the great missionary to India, died? When God took one great evangelist from this world, He replenished it with another.'

A mighty roar thundered outside the church. 'What is that noise?' Charles asked Dr. Fletcher.

'That noise, Charles, is two thousand people upset about not being able to come inside. The police have sealed off the doors. This is the biggest event in London.'

'I have to admit,' Charles said, 'I'm a little nervous.'

'Don't worry, Susannah is a fine young woman. She will make a perfect pastor's wife.'

'Romance has never really been a part of my life,' he muttered. 'I hope I'm good at it!'

Dr. Fletcher saw the anxiety in Charles' eyes and smiled. 'When was the first time you pronounced your love for her?' he asked.

The memory relaxed Charles. 'It was June 10th, 1854. Queen Victoria gave a ceremony for the opening of the Crystal Palace at Sydenham, previously located in Hyde Park. A group of us from the church went to the opening ceremony. I had brought a book of love poetry with me, just in case a need would arise.' Charles winked. 'And a need did arise! The Crystal Palace was beautiful that day, but not as beautiful as the girl sitting beside me. As people marched through the palace, playing all kinds of music, I handed her the poetry and asked her to read a verse.'

"'What did it say?'

'You have to understand, I ploughed through many poems to find it. It needed to be a perfect poem.

> 'If thou art to have a wife of thy youth,
>   she is now living on the earth;
>   Therefore think of her
>   and pray for her well!'"

While she was reading the words, I whispered softly in her ear, "Susannah, do you pray for he who is to be your husband?" And from that moment on, she has not stopped praying for me.'

'What a wonderful story!' Rev. Fletcher said. 'She is not the only woman praying for you. Before the ceremony, your mother told me how she used to spend hours on her knees pleading with God to bless you and give you godly wisdom. You would not be standing here today had it not been for your mother's unceasing prayers.'

Charles looked over at her. 'It was true,' he thought. 'All those nights when I awoke from terrifying nightmares to find her on her knees in the kitchen. I suppose no one ever makes it through life alone. There are always friends who encourage us, uncles and aunts who instruct us, godly parents in the background praying on our behalf. Thank you, God, for listening to my mother's prayers.'

The sanctuary, which rattled with noise, suddenly silenced. The back doors of the chapel opened. Charles' jaw dropped. There was his bride, standing before his eyes. She was breathtaking!

Susannah met Charles at the altar. 'This is the moment I have waited for my whole life,' he thought. Susannah's face was obscured behind a thin, white veil, but Charles could see her tears. After two long years of chaperoned courting, they were about to have one another for themselves.

Charles and Susannah faced Dr. Fletcher, who was giving a brief sermon on the importance of marriage, but Charles, who very much loved sermons, couldn't concentrate on anything but his new wife.

'And what God has joined together,' Dr. Fletcher concluded, 'let no one put asunder!' He looked at Charles. 'Do you, Charles, take Susannah to be your wife, in sickness and in health, until death do you part?'

'I do!' he bellowed.

'And Susannah, do you take Charles to be your husband, in sickness and in health, until death do you part?'

She said, 'Oh, yes, I do!'

'Then by the power vested in me, I pronounce you man and wife,' Rev. Fletcher declared. 'I now introduce you to Mr. and Mrs. Charles Spurgeon!'

Charles took his bride's hand and marched down the aisle. As they burst through the doors of the chapel, they were greeted with the commotion of two thousand people. Charles could not believe his eyes. Policeman kept the people from crushing them as they ran to the getaway carriage.

Opening the carriage door, Charles helped Susannah into her seat. For his sweetness, she gave him a crowd-pleasing kiss. Charles wasn't used to public displays of affection, but he didn't complain. The newly-weds were alone at last. A final wave goodbye, through the window, and the carriage drove down the street.

After an hour or so (no one was keeping track), Susannah looked into the eyes of her husband.

'Where are we going?'

Charles Spurgeon

'Ah, wifey,' he said. 'It is not customary for the bride to know the location of the honeymoon.'

Susannah persisted. 'Then perhaps I might change that custom today!' She leaned in and gently kissed him on the lips.

Susannah's quick wit and intellect had always impressed Charles. 'Woman,' he said, 'your methods are persuasive, indeed.' But Charles would not disclose the information quite yet. Susannah moved in for another kiss, but Charles beat her to it, whispering the name of the destination in her ear.

'Paris?' Susannah squealed. 'I love France! This will be the best honeymoon ever!'

Charles reached into his coat pocket and pulled out a folded piece of paper. 'I wrote you something last night,' he said, placing it in her hands.

'A poem!' Susannah said. She loved Charles' poetry. Her eyes followed the lines, savouring every syllable.

> 'He who chose worlds before,
> must reign in our hearts alone,
> We fondly believe we shall adore,
> together before His throne.'
> – C.H. Spurgeon

Susannah laid her head against Charles' shoulder. 'I love you,' she whispered. The whole day had been a blur to her – the wedding, the crowds, and now the carriage ride. For the first time in her life, she felt protected. 'Maybe my aunt was right,' she mused. 'Maybe this story will have a happy ending after all.'

A Broken Balcony

Mr. and Mrs. Charles Spurgeon's house,
Nightingale Lane, Clapham – 1856

'Wake up, dear husband; it is almost time for the service to start.' Susannah gently laid her palm on Charles' forehead.

He yawned and opened his eyes. 'How long have I been sleeping?'

'All afternoon. I was going to wake you earlier, but I wanted you to get all the rest you could. You have never preached in the Surrey Music Hall before. It can seat up to ten thousand people, and some are predicting twice that many will come to hear you preach.'

'Twenty thousand people?' Charles asked. 'I hope my voice will hold.'

'God gives us exactly what we need when we need it,' she replied, quoting an old sermon of his.

Charles' suit was ironed and Susannah now helped him to get into it. Charles was only twenty-two years old and didn't own many suits. He always used his money to help others who needed it more.

Placing a top hat on his head, Charles took his wife by the arm. Less than a month before, Susannah had given birth to twin sons – Charles and Thomas. She had not yet fully recovered from the delivery, but she was not about to let Charles leave without her. They walked outside to the carriage.

The Surrey Music Hall was rectangular in shape and rounded on the edges. It was situated on a spacious, green piece of land. Beside it, a blue lake reflected the four magnificent towers spiralling up from each of the four corners of the building. Architecturally, it was magnificent.

'I hope everyone will be able to fit inside,' Susannah said.

Charles shared her thought. 'This building was originally designed for circuses and theatrical performances. Lions, tigers, and elephants are exhibited here throughout the year. I've even read about children riding large sea turtles by the river.'

'Has anyone ever preached here before?' she asked.

'Not to my knowledge,' Charles replied. He knew this was going to be a daunting challenge. 'People eat picnics here and watch fireworks explode. Preaching will certainly be a new event. But New Park Street Baptist Church can no longer seat all the new members. This is our only option and since our church will be meeting here from now on, let's pray it won't be a zoo in there.'

Susannah touched his hand. Usually, this eased his nerves, but tonight the anxiety was on his face.

'Everything will be fine' she said.

Charles had his doubts.

'Do you remember the first time you ever preached – in Teversham?'

Charles remembered.

'You told me how nervous you were because you did not know what you were going to say or how you were going to say it. But when you stood to preach, God gave you a peace. He will do the same again for you tonight.'

Charles nodded. His concern was more for the safety of the crowds than the status of his sermon. That many people in one place could be dangerous!

Susannah wove her fingers through his. 'God has not brought you this far only to abandon you now.'

A group of deacons helped Charles and Susannah out of their carriage. They shook his hand and said, 'We will be taking you and your wife into the music hall through a secret side entrance. We don't want the mob to see you before the service begins. Your popularity in London has increased, but so have your enemies. We don't want to take any chances tonight.'

Charles paused and looked at the group of deacons. 'Whenever the gospel of Jesus Christ is touching lives and saving souls,' he said, 'we can be sure the devil is working diligently to stop our progress. It is good, dear gentlemen, to remind the devil that we are his enemies. And we should expect that he will remind us that he is ours.'

Charles, Susannah, and the deacons entered the interior of the music hall. Its grandeur left them breathless. The entire ceiling was built from rounded glass. Crystal chandeliers hung from beams above the floor below. The magnitude of the place was mesmerizing. Charles kissed Susannah one last time before climbing up the large platform to his seat. Susannah followed the deacons.

Charles looked out across the massive crowd of people. Thousands looked back at him. Some were poor and dressed in rags; others were wealthy. Some were rude and impatient, eager to get the service underway; others sat quietly in their seats, praying for the preacher. When all the seats had been filled, the empty spaces crowded with people. They stood wherever they could. Many stood in aisles, others sat on the floor. The walls and balconies ached under the weight of the congregation. Its capacity was quickly reaching the limit. Shoulder to shoulder, everyone squeezed together. The noise was deafening.

'How can I preach against such a mighty roar?' Charles thought. 'Father,' he prayed. 'Help me communicate your truth and salvation to these people. They seem to be like sheep without a shepherd, wandering in from the wilderness. Give me the boldness of Elijah, the tenderness of David, and the simplicity of John the Baptist.'

Susannah whispered to the deacon sitting beside her, 'When was the last time someone preached to this many people in London?'

Charles Spurgeon

The deacon, who was many years older than Susannah, thought for a moment. 'Madam, I believe this is the largest crowd ever gathered to hear a single preacher since the days of George Whitefield, over a hundred years ago. Your husband is making history.'

Chaos and disorder flooded the auditorium. Thousands stood outside, wanting to hear bits of his sermon through the open windows. Charles oozed with anxiety. 'With such a large number of people,' he thought from the platform, 'if something goes wrong, it will be difficult to maintain safety, order, and civility.'

'Pray hard for him,' Susannah told the deacon. 'I have never seen him so burdened.'

Charles checked his watch. It was 6 o'clock — time to start. Ten thousand people were still pushing and screaming to get inside, but if the service did not begin now, it might not begin at all.

'God help me,' Charles prayed, climbing up the towering pulpit. 'I hate heights!'

'Ever since he was a boy,' Susannah whispered to the deacon, 'heights have bothered him. His grandfather told him stories about people falling into eternal abysses. Even today, he avoids ledges and railings.'

Charles clinched the pulpit. He not only hated heights, but he also hated being so far away from the people to whom he was preaching. Charles enjoyed looking his congregation in the eye. He was, after all, an artist. If the eyes were the window into the soul and he was, by calling, a soul preacher, he needed to see their eyes. He needed to know how they were feeling, how they were responding to the tones of his voice, and how his sermon could better relate to their individual situations. 'Lord, I feel so disconnected from them,' Charles prayed, squinting his eyes to see their faces. The organist was but a dot in the distance.

Suddenly, all the chatter dissipated. Everyone anticipated the first word Charles Spurgeon would say. All eyes were on him. Hearts and souls were depending on him. His legs began to shake – they supported a heavy heart.

CREAK. A loud noise ripped through the building, like fresh wood splintering into fragments.

'What was that?' People looked around, but no one could identify the source of the sound. The deacons were as clueless as Charles. CREAK, CREAK, CREAK. The sound strengthened and grew into a noisy mixture of bending metal, twisting wood, and crumbling concrete. 'Something is very wrong!'

It would happen at any moment – something would snap and there would not be a thing in the world Charles could do to prevent it. It was just a matter of time. No one knew how close to danger they were, but suddenly, in the calm before the storm, Susannah knew.

'Please God,' she prayed, looking over her shoulder, 'not the balcony!'

The noise grew more disturbing – almost demonic – as it jeered, taunted, and provoked the people to frenzy.

'Perhaps these sounds are normal for a building that is adjusting to a large crowd,' Charles reasoned. 'It was designed to hold thousands of people, and I don't want to cause any alarm by asking anyone to leave. That alone might cause more harm than good.'

'Turn in your hymnal,' Charles said, 'to page three hundred and–'

CREAK, CREAK, CREAK. 'Uh oh,' Charles thought. CRASH! He heard the gasps of horror coming from the balcony. And when the beams that held the weight collapsed, Charles's greatest fear became a present reality. People began to fall, just like in his grandfather's stories.

'The place is falling apart!' someone yelled. 'Run for your life!'

'We're all going to die!' another screamed. 'Save the women and children!'

The noise was frightening. As the balcony floor began to twist and convulse beneath their feet, people began to fall over the railings. Charles could not move. His legs were stiff, his knees were locked, and his body would not respond. He saw little children fall onto the crowd below. It was a nightmare.

Several men from the balcony fell on top of Susannah. She was knocked to the floor and hit her face against a chair. The deacons sitting beside her tried to push the crowd away so she could stand up, but it was no use. She was already ill from the pregnancy and delivery, and she could not escape the weight upon her.

No scene could have frightened a husband more. It was a torment worse than torture and Charles stood frozen, paralysed with pain. The ground seemed to be giving way, sending dozens to their deaths.

'I have to do something!' he thought. 'Do not panic!' Charles screamed at the top of his lungs. 'Remain calm! Exit the auditorium in an orderly fashion!' The more he pleaded, the more they panicked, pushed, kicked, scratched, clawed, bit, and fought to get out of the Surrey Music Hall. Thousands of people were still trying to get inside the auditorium, wanting to take the seats of those who were running out for their lives.

'Fire!' someone shouted. 'There's a fire! We're all going to be burned alive!'

Charles could not see any fire from the pulpit, but he didn't doubt it. It was sheer madness, and Charles could take no more. The last thing Charles remembered before collapsing in a faint was his dear wife completely buried beneath the violent crowd. Charles' legs weakened. His head lightened. The church seemed to spin. And he, too, fell backwards into ... nothing.

* * *

Mr. and Mrs. Spurgeon's house, Nightingale Lane, Clapham – the next evening

Susannah stirred a cup of tea as she read an article in the evening newspaper:

'Yesterday evening, at the Surrey Garden Music Hall, a tragedy beyond tragedies occurred. It was a horrible event led by the lunatic, Mr. Charles Spurgeon, a preacher who hurls damnation at his congregation. He watched unsympathetically as hundreds of people escaped from the auditorium with barely the shirts on their back. Men and women clawed one another, fighting for their lives to escape the ghastly scene. Mr. Spurgeon, who has no formal theological education, watched from the safety of his pulpit as people deteriorated into animals before his eyes. Since the Surrey Music Hall is known for such animalistic displays, it seemed to be a fitting performance for London's young, reckless preacher.'

A tear landed on the newspaper and bled through the ink. 'My husband must never see this.' She tore the newspaper in half. 'The preacher that London once loved has now become its enemy.'

Susannah checked on Charles, who had been sleeping since the tragedy. As she opened the door, a beam of light pierced the darkness of the room and struck Charles on his face. His eyes were already open, staring blankly at the ceiling.

'Charles?' she said, walking over to him. 'Can you hear me?' She touched his cheeks. They burned with fever.

'Susie, is that you?'

'Yes, dear, it is.' She rested the cup of hot tea on his night stand.

'I just had the worst nightmare,' Charles said. 'People were falling, dying and screaming. Little children, Susie, were trampled by the crowds. Clothes tore from shoulders …there was so much blood … so much pain … so much chaos. Thank God it was only a dream!'

Susannah's heart skipped a beat. 'He doesn't know!'

'What's the matter, Susie?'

She said nothing, her eyes glued to the ground.

'Susannah?'

'Charles, it was not a dream,' she said.

'Of course it was.'

Susannah sighed, her face downcast. A deep gash extended from the bottom of her eye to the top of her lip.

'Susie, what happened to your face?' Charles asked.

'Don't you remember?'

Charles was confused. 'Remember what?' Moments ticked by, one after the other. Charles searched his mind for memory … and then he remembered.

Charles screamed and jolted in his bed, knocking the cup of hot tea onto the floor. Porcelain shattered into a thousand pieces. 'It was real!' he yelled. 'Oh no, Susie, I remember everything! It was real.'

Susannah burst into tears and wrapped her arms around him. 'You passed out,' she sobbed, 'and fell down the stairs of the pulpit.'

Charles shuddered violently in his bed. 'Was anyone killed?' he asked.

'It was not your fault,' Susannah said, avoiding the question. 'It was out of your control!'

'How many?' he asked, trembling.

Susannah could not reply. She put her head on his chest and wept bitterly.

'Susie, how many people lost their lives?'

She knew her answer would crush him. 'Seven people died, and twenty-eight were seriously injured.'

Charles was devastated. 'I am a murderer,' he said, putting his head on the pillow. 'Please leave me alone right now, Susie. I need to be alone.'

'Charles, you are not a murderer! You did everything in your power to help them. There were just too many people, and too much weight, and –'

'Leave me be,' he said. 'Just for the night.' Susannah knew it would only take a night to sever his sanity. She recognized the tone in his voice – it was the tone of a defeated man returning from battle without his victory. Susannah bent down to pick up the jagged pieces of porcelain scattered under the bed, but there were too many of them. Maybe for the night, they needed to remain broken. She walked to the door and then turned around.

'You are a great preacher, Charles Haddon Spurgeon. Don't you dare let the devil win the war within you!' Susannah closed the door and disappeared.

Father to the Orphans

Metropolitan Tabernacle, London –
Sunday morning, 1877

Charles was forty-three years old. His eyes were wiser than before, his face seasoned by life's stormy weather. It had been over twenty years since the balcony at the Surrey Music Hall collapsed, yet the memory was fresh in Spurgeon's dreams. He never recovered from the tragic incident. Every time a large crowd assembled, his pulse palpitated and his body felt paralysed.

Charles stood before his congregation. 'Our text for the morning is found in the Old Testament book of Habakkuk. "Oh God, revive thy work." When the balcony collapsed at the Surrey Music Hall, I sank deep into the valley of depression. It was the lowest moment of my life. For weeks I dwelt in isolation, finding no comfort in food, sleep, or Scripture.'

Susannah closed her eyes. The memory disturbed her. The incident had so emotionally overwhelmed her husband, that she doubted if he would ever recover.

'But one day,' Charles continued, 'as I was walking through my garden, this text came to my mind. "Revive thy work, oh God." It hit me like a load of heavy bricks –

preaching is not my work, preaching is God's work! God called me to this task. God supplies the resources for this business. As I sat underneath the shade of a tree, I raised my head to heaven and prayed, "Oh God, revive thy work. Only you can do it, I am much too weak. Only you can patch the broken pieces of my life. Only you can drive away my depression."'

Charles paused. He looked into his congregation's eyes. Many of them bore the scars of tragedies on their faces. 'Maybe you are sitting here this morning,' he softly said, 'and you are struggling for strength to survive. With David, you are walking through the valley of the shadow of death. I have good news for you, dear soul. Jesus Christ is in the business of new beginnings. If God begins a work in you, He is able, willing, and competent to complete it. God never draws out the blueprints for a project He is incapable of accomplishing! Dear soul, pray that God will revive His work in your life.'

Charles concluded the worship service with a hymn and a prayer. He walked back to his pastor's study which was in the church, praying that the Holy Spirit had used his words to encourage his congregation.

There was a knock at the door. 'Come in,' Charles said.

A deacon entered. 'Rev. Spurgeon, you have a visitor. He attended our service this morning and demands to speak with you. I asked for his name, but he refused my request. Should I send him away?'

Charles Spurgeon

Charles closed the book he was reading. 'Our Saviour never turned people away,' he said. 'Nor shall we. Show him in.'

The stranger walked through the door. He was tall and trim. His shoes sparkled with expense; his hat was London's finest. There was something familiar about him. The stranger entered the room, closed the door and locked it.

'What are you doing?' Charles inquired, standing to his feet.

The stranger did not reply. Step after step, he approached the desk where Charles was standing. The hat on his head prevented Charles from seeing his eyes.

'Who is this intruder?' Spurgeon wondered.

Tension filled the room. 'Have we met, sir?' Charles asked.

There was no reply.

'Do you wish to harm me?'

With the eloquence of an athlete, the stranger jumped into action and planted his fist firmly beneath Charles' rib cage. Charles doubled over from the blow, surprised by the assault. But somehow, he was not too surprised. It was a familiar punch.

'Henry? Is that you?'

The stranger erupted in laughter and removed his hat.

'Just like old times, huh Charles?' Henry said, helping him up.

The Prince of Preachers

It was like old times. Too much like old times. 'It is much easier to hit an old fat man than a young fat one,' Charles said. 'There's more of me to punch, now.'

Henry gave Charles a big hug and took a good look at him. 'Time has taken its toll on you, old friend.'

'The years have been kinder to you,' Charles replied.

Henry looked around the pastor's study. 'You have quite a ministry here,' he said. 'I always knew God would give you the desires of your heart. While I was listening to you preach this morning, I remembered your first sermon in Teversham – so long ago. Remember how nervous you were?'

Charles remembered. 'I have good memories of those days, those first fruits in the ministry – the dark open fields, the long dirty roads, the green Cambridge scenery.'

'Your sermon was really good.' Henry said. 'You still have the same spark I remember. How did God bring you to this church in London?'

Charles pulled up a chair for Henry. 'When I moved to London, I was the pastor of New Park Street Baptist Church. Eventually, so many people came that we were forced to build another church. Construction on the Metropolitan Tabernacle began in 1859. It was an expensive project. By the grace of God, we funded it without sinking into debt. But enough about me, Henry. How have you spent the last twenty-seven years?'

'I left Cambridge shortly after you became the pastor in Waterbeach. I wanted to study law, so I moved to London to pursue my degree.'

'What about that girl? The one you kept sneaking out to see ... ' Charles asked. 'Did you marry her?'

Henry smiled. 'No, I met someone else, but it's a long story.'

'Shorten it for me,' Charles said, eager to know who Henry had fallen in love with.

Henry acquiesced. 'I have you to thank for that really ... you once encouraged a young woman to attend church and read *The Pilgrim's Progress* ...'

'Mary?' Charles exclaimed. 'She had the reddest hair I have ever seen – and lots of freckles.' Charles was speechless.

'She may have started with very little education – but it's a different story now. She's a lovely Christian. It didn't take me long to ask her to marry me!'

Charles shook his head in happy disbelief.

'What about you, Charles? Who did you marry?'

Charles took a picture frame off his desk and handed it to Henry. 'Her name is Susannah. She is the most amazing, talented, supportive woman in the world. She is a jewel among women.'

Henry pulled out a small package from his pocket and handed it to Charles. 'This is for you,' he said. 'When I told Mary I was coming to hear you preach, she insisted that I give this to you.'

Charles untied the bow and tore off the wrapping.

'She said you would like it.'

Charles grinned. He did like it, indeed. The inscription read, 'To Charles, the man who inspired me to read. Thank you for keeping the ending a secret. Love, Mary.'

Charles placed the copy of *The Pilgrim's Progress* on his desk. 'What does Mary do these days?'

Henry was so proud of her. 'She is a teacher.'

'A teacher?' Charles said. 'Who does she teach?'

'As you know, there is such a need in London for ministry with children. Orphans are everywhere.'

Charles knew. He loved the orphans of London very much. 'It breaks my heart to see them,' he said. 'Sometimes they sneak into our worship services in the winter, trying to get warm. They don't have the love of parents, nor the comforts of home. Many sweep chimneys for a living and often die prematurely because of the miserable conditions. How long has Mary been working with them?'

'Every Saturday she gathers some together and teaches them to read and write. It gives them something to live for.'

'I would love it if our church could assist these orphans in some way.' Charles sighed.

Henry paused to think. 'Perhaps there is something …' he said. 'Right now I am working with a widow named Mrs. Hillyard, who just inherited a large sum of money. She wants to give £20,000 to the service of God, but she does not know how to channel it. She asked me if I knew of a need to which she could contribute her donation.'

Charles thought for a moment. 'If there's anyone who needs that money in this city, it's the orphans.' Charles had an idea. 'What if we could build an orphanage for them?'

'An orphanage?' Henry said.

'We could build it near our church. It would meet their physical and emotional needs, but most importantly, we could teach them the Bible and provide a Christian environment for them to grow up in.'

There was enthusiasm in the thought, and Henry went with it. 'Charles, I want to tell you something. When we were students together in Cambridge, I revered you as a brilliant biblical scholar. You communicated the most complicated theological doctrines in the plainest of language, so even people like me could understand it. You moulded eternal truths for simple minds. *Plain Advice for Plain People* – the book you wrote when you were in your early twenties – made such a difference in my life. You always had a passion for underprivileged people. An orphanage would be a natural extension of your pastoral ministry and your pastoral heart. You would be a father to them, Charles – the father they never had.'

Charles needed time for this idea to incubate. 'God might have sent you here this morning for this very reason,' he said.

Henry smiled. 'You never did believe in accidents, did you?'

Charles shook his head. 'There are no accidents with God. Let me talk to God about this idea, and if He permits us to build this orphanage, I will let you know.'

Henry handed Charles a card. 'If you need to write to me, this is my address.'

Charles stood to his feet and showed Henry to the door. 'Thank you so much for stopping by.'

As Charles opened the door, Henry put his hat back on. His eyes were again concealed.

'You should have seen your face,' he said. 'You were scared out of your wits!'

Charles grinned.

'You haven't changed a bit, old friend.'

Thomas was twelve years old. It wasn't easy being a preacher's kid – especially if your dad was Charles Haddon Spurgeon. The expectations were extremely high. Whenever he and his brother, Charles, got into trouble, the whole world found out about it.

'Dad, are you coming with us?' Thomas asked, getting into the carriage.

'No, I'm going for a walk, boys,' he said. 'Make sure you get your mother home safely. I will meet you there in a little while.' Charles kissed his wife goodbye and began to walk down the street.

'Is something bothering Dad?' Thomas asked.

Susannah touched his shoulder. 'Your father is fine,' she said. 'He just needs some time alone with the Lord.'

Thomas was sceptical.

The horses jolted the carriage into motion. 'Have I ever told you what your father said about these horses?' Susannah asked.

The twin boys shook their heads.

'As you know,' she began, 'your father loves these animals. Every Sunday they faithfully pull us to church. One day, a man came up to your father and criticized him for making the horses work so hard on Sunday, the day of the Lord. Your father never likes criticism and he often uses his humour to redirect assaults. When he heard this man's complaint, Charles looked at him and said, 'These horses are in no great sin for pulling me to church every Sunday. You see, my horses are Jewish and they celebrate their Sabbath on Saturday."

Thomas and his brother exploded in laughter. 'Dad really said that?' Tom asked.

'Boys, if only you knew half the things your father has said.' Susannah smiled.

Charles strolled aimlessly through the streets of London. He had no destination in mind – there was no hurry. He passed young boys selling newspapers and shouting, 'The invention of the telephone is changing the world. Read all about it!'

Block after block, Charles walked, waiting for a heavenly word from the Lord – a phone call from his father. 'What would you have me do about the orphanage?' he prayed. 'There are so many children in this city who need your healing touch in their lives. Give me a sign – a crystal clear sign.'

After crossing the Thames, Charles felt a shot of pain rush through his knees. They had never been strong knees like Henry's, but recently, they would often cause him to collapse in excruciating pain. Charles sat down on a bench.

'Excuse me, sir, you can't sit there.'

Charles could not figure out where the voice was coming from.

'I said, you cannot sit here!'

'And why not?' Charles asked. 'The earth is the Lord's, and the fullness thereof.'

Suddenly, a child appeared from behind the bench. 'You can't sit here because you haven't paid the bench tax.'

'The bench tax?' Charles asked. 'I have never heard of a tax like that!'

The child persisted.

'If you want to sit on my bench, you must pay the tax.'

Charles was intrigued. 'And how much is the tax, young man?'

'It depends on how long you sit.'

Charles Spurgeon

'I see,' Charles said. 'Well, let me see how much money I have.' He reached into his pocket and pulled out a few pence. 'How long will this buy me?'

'Five minutes,' the child replied, 'and no longer.'

Charles was impressed with the child's cleverness. 'I will pay this tax to you on one condition,' he said. The child was not accustomed to conditions.

'I will pay you this money if you will sit with me on the bench.'

The boy agreed. 'Fair enough,' he said, snatching the money.

'So where do you live?' Charles asked.

There was no reply.

'You are breaking your end of the deal,' Charles said.

'You did not say I had to answer any questions while I sat on the bench with you,' the boy said. 'Questions will cost you extra, mister.'

Charles smiled and reached into his pocket. 'I am willing to pay for the answers,' he said, handing him another penny.

'I am an orphan,' he said. 'I sweep chimneys.'

'What's your name?' Charles asked. The boy did not reply until Charles handed him another coin.

He coughed. 'My name is Edward.'

'Well, Edward, my name is Charles Spurgeon and I am a pastor.'

Charles did not have many coins left, so he decided to ask important questions. 'Have you ever been to church?'

'Once,' Edward said, 'when I was young ... before my parents sent me away.'

'What do you remember about it?'

He paused. 'There was singing – like angels.'

Charles looked at Edward. He seemed too mature for his youth. His arms were small and dirty. His clothes were simple, tattered, unwashed. His eyes lacked childlike vigour – their sparkle had long since vanished. 'How often do you clean chimneys?' he asked.

'Every day,' he replied. 'Well, sometimes Master gives us a day off. In fact, on my day off, I'm learning to read!'

'And who is your teacher?'

Edward did not know her name. 'She has long, red hair,' he said with a cough.

'Mary,' Charles thought.

Charles hated the sound of Edward's cough. He knew that chimney sweeps inhale large quantities of soot—often fatal amounts. 'Edward,' he said, 'if you could do anything in the world, what would you do?'

Edward had never been asked that question before.

'Anything in the world?' he asked.

'Anything,' Charles said. 'No matter how much the cost.'

Edward looked into Charles' eyes. A hint of hope almost broke through. 'I have always wanted one thing ...' he said. 'At night, when everyone is sleeping, I dream of it.'

'What do you dream of, Edward?

'Boats,' he replied. 'Big, white, beautiful boats, floating in fresh, salty sea water. I would have a large crew. And they would obey my orders.'

'Ah. And what would you name a ship like that?' Charles asked.

Edward had no name. 'Do all boats have to have names?'

'Well, good boats have names,' Charles said. 'A boat without a name is like a dog without a collar – it could belong to anybody. Edward, what would you name your boat?'

Edward's mind searched through all the words he knew until he found the perfect one. 'Liberty. She would have large, white open sails that would blow her into the blue unknown – away from chimneys, cities, and soot.' Edward smiled at the thought. 'And there would be only one rule on my boat: No one would ever be allowed to cough.'

Charles' heart broke, but he forced a smile. 'A boat like that would go very far,' he said. 'Especially if you were the captain.'

Edward thought so.

'I want you to do something for me,' Charles said, reaching into his briefcase. Charles scribbled a quick note on a piece of paper and sealed it in an envelope. 'Will you run an errand for me, Edward?'

'Mister, it'll cost you.'

Charles expected as much. 'Oh, this is a very important errand,' he said. 'I am willing to pay top price.'

Charles took a crisp bill from his pocket and handed it to Edward, who quickly put it in his pocket. 'There is a store down the street,' he said. 'It has a big, blue sign above its door. Do you know the one?'

'I know the one.'

Charles handed the envelope to Edward. 'Give this to the clerk behind the counter – he's my friend.'

Edward jumped off the bench. 'Your message will be delivered faster than lightning.' Edward was overwhelmed with duty. No one had ever paid him so much money in all his life. He ran down the street as fast as his little legs could carry him. Charles watched him disappear around the bend.

Charles' knees felt better, so he stood again. Suddenly, a piece of paper fell from his pocket and landed on the ground. 'What is this?' he thought, bending down to pick it up. It was Henry's card. Charles smiled. 'Thank you, Lord,' he prayed. 'That was just the sign I needed.'

Edward arrived at the store, out of breath and weary from the run. He opened the door and walked inside. A clerk stood behind the counter, just as Charles had predicted. Rushing up to him, Edward placed the envelope in his hands. 'This is for you, sir.'

'Who is this from?' the clerk asked.

'This is from Mr. Spurgeon.'

Charles Spurgeon

The name alone brought a smile to the clerk's face.

'Thank you, son,' he said, patting him on the head. Having completed his mission, Edward turned and ran out the door.

'Come back!' yelled the clerk. He chased after the child.

Edward was terrified. 'Am I in trouble? Maybe Mr. Spurgeon is getting me back for the bench tax I charged him.' He froze in his tracks, and the clerk dragged him back inside the store.

'Wait right here, young lad,' the clerk said. 'And don't you dare leave!' Edward waited.

The clerk disappeared behind the counter. Minutes passed and the silence grew deafening in Edward's ears. He considered running away. 'If I left now, no one could catch me.'

Before he had time to plan his escape, the clerk returned, carrying an unusual object in his hands. Edward examined it. It was white, curved, and had a mast – a boat!

Edward was speechless. He glued his eyes to the beautiful ship. It certainly looked seaworthy. 'Wait a minute,' Edward thought. He looked around the shop. 'This is not an ordinary store.' Stuffed animals lined the walls – dragons, tigers, elephants. Castles, candy, and cartoons were scattered throughout the aisles. Small cars and moving trains filled the floor. 'This is a toy store.'

The clerk set the model boat on the counter. 'According to this letter,' he said, reading the words again, 'this boat belongs to you.'

Edward's eyes grew wide as he ran his hands along the port side of the wooden ship.

'It is one of our very finest,' the clerk said, proudly.

Edwards grabbed the miniature captain's wheel and turned the rudder. It swung from side to side. 'It's perfect,' he said.

'Well, almost perfect …' the clerk said, reading the last sentence on the note. Spurgeon's handwriting was difficult to read. 'Ah, of course,' he said, reaching into the drawer beneath the counter. He pulled out a tiny paintbrush and dipped it into a jar of black ink. With a steady hand, he painted a word onto the side of the ship. 'That should do.'

Edward waited while the paint dried. It seemed like eternity. Finally, the clerk turned the boat. He could barely read, but Edward traced the curvy letters with his eyes. They were the most beautiful letters he had ever seen – they were his letters. He pronounced the word in his mind before declaring it with his lips … Liberty.

Charles woke up covered with sweat and trembling. The pillow beneath his neck was wet with perspiration.

'Are you alright?' Susannah asked, awakened by the movement. 'Another nightmare?'

Charles nodded. 'It was terrible,' he whispered. 'Hundreds of orphans were running – falling off cliffs. Their faces were black from soot, and … and they all died.'

Charles Spurgeon

By now, Susannah knew exactly how to comfort her husband after a nightmare and she had lots of practice. Wrapping her arms around him, she held Charles closely to her side. 'It wasn't real,' she reminded him.

Charles thought of Edward. 'Susie, I met a child today. He was an orphan.'

'You've met lots of orphans,' she said, rocking him back and forth.

'Yes, but this one was different. It was like God sent him to me for a reason. I think we can help them, Susie.'

'How?' she asked.

Charles knew how. 'I'll be back in a minute,' he said, jumping out of bed.

In his study, Charles frantically searched for a piece of paper. He found one, and the light of the lantern flickered shadows against it. Charles squinted as he wrote.

Dear Henry,
Greetings in the name of our Lord and Saviour, Jesus Christ. It has become crystal clear to me that we should open the orphanage. Tell Mrs. Hillyard I would love to meet with her to discuss the details of the project. John 14:18.
God bless,
C. H. Spurgeon

Charles folded the letter and went back to bed. He slipped beneath the sheets. 'We can save them,' he said.

'How?'

The Prince of Preachers

'When I was a boy,' Charles whispered, 'I was searching through my grandfather's attic and found something I will never forget. Right next to *The Pilgrim's Progress* was a bottle and inside the bottle was an apple. The apple was red because of the yellow liquid preserving it. As I studied the apple, I could not understand how it fitted inside the bottle. The bottle neck was far too narrow for the large apple to slide through.'

Susannah's eyes grew heavy and lost their focus, but she forced her ears to pay attention.

'One day, I asked my grandfather how the apple got in the bottle. He told me to think about it for a day. I thought for hours, trying to solve the problem. Early the next morning, I ran into his room and demanded an answer.'

Susannah closed her eyes and her breathing grew rhythmic.

'My grandfather took me into the kitchen. He took a small apple – a baby apple still connected to its limb – and slid it into a bottle. It fitted right in! Over the next few weeks we watered the limb and the baby apple matured into a ripe piece of fruit. Not a thing in the world could hurt or harm it because of the glass walls of protection.' Charles paused. He himself was growing sleepy. 'If we can shelter the orphans while they are young,' he mumbled, 'they might survive.'

Susannah did not respond – she was fast asleep. 'Revive thy work in this city, oh Lord,' Charles prayed, joining her in her dreams.

Memories from Mentone

Mentone, France – 1889

A white, wooden chair rested in the sand. It was a good chair – the best, according to fifty-five-year old Charles. Waves crashed against the French shore. This was his favourite place in all the world. During the coldest part of the winter, he escaped the snowy weather of London to relax at the peaceful resort in Mentone. Lush gardens surrounded his hotel, the Beau Rivage. The hot sun refreshed his spirit, calmed his depression, and gave Charles time to write, study, and think – luxuries that he lacked in London.

The sea smelled salty in his nose. Often, Charles came here in his mind. When the London newspapers criticized him or when his work load overwhelmed him, he would simply close his eyes and sit on this beach, feeling the cool sand ooze between his toes, watching the crystal blue water foam against the mossy rocks.

In the distance, boat masts poked into the sky. 'That would make a fine picture,' Charles thought, reaching for a pencil. Sketching was an old hobby of his, that had never really died. His frantic schedule prevented him from drawing as much as he wanted to. Charles preached as often as ten times a week, each message a new one. But from time to time he carved out little moments to draw. This was one of those times. With precise strokes, Charles sketched the horizon line in the margins of the newspaper he was reading. Every detail that paradise could produce was seen and replicated. As he sketched the shoreline, a gentle gust of wind blew the newspaper from his hands. It rolled across the sand and out of sight. Charles didn't care; he was too busy savouring the warm breeze, the lush palm trees, and the peaceful atmosphere.

'Pardon me, Mr. Spurgeon,' a young hotel worker said. His French accent was strong. 'Does this belong to you?'

Charles looked at him. He was holding the newspaper that had blown away.

'Why yes, thank you,' he said, catching a glimpse of the front page: EIFFEL TOWER'S CONSTRUCTION ALMOST COMPLETE. A black and white photograph of the half-built structure filled the page. 'Have you been to Paris to see it?' he asked the man.

The hotel worker shook his head. 'No, I've been too busy. People call it the eighth wonder of the world – the tallest building ever built.'

Charles smiled. 'It seems we are always reaching higher into heaven. We want to be a part of something bigger than ourselves, greater than ourselves. You know, the first major building project in the Bible was a tower—the tower of Babel.'

Charles Spurgeon

The hotel worker nodded. 'Spoken like the words of a true preacher,' he said. 'And were it not for the tower of Babel, you and I would speak the same language.'

Charles was impressed. 'So, you are familiar with the story?'

'It's one of my favourites,' he said. The hotel worker smiled at Charles. 'And Mentone must be one of your favourites too ... we have seen you here quite a few times now.'

'Oh yes,' Charles replied. 'I come here every winter. I call this land my "sunny south".'

'Queen Victoria stays at this hotel when she comes to Mentone,' the hotel worker said. 'In fact, most famous people like you come here.'

Charles didn't like the word famous. He never sought after fame or attention; it just landed in his lap. Charles shook his head. 'Let me tell you a secret. In the past, there have been great men – Martin Luther, John Calvin, George Whitefield. They were like mountains on the horizon. Everyone could see them. They built their ministries upon the foundation of Jesus. They have gone before us, blazing a trail beneath our feet.'

The hotel worker followed the word picture.

'Now, God does not call many men to be mountains,' Charles continued. 'He calls most of us to be simple, smooth stones where weary pilgrims may rest, when they walk through the valley of the shadow of death. We should not view ourselves too highly lest our mountains become volcanoes, erupting with pride and self righteousness. We should not seek to be great; we should seek to be faithful.'

The hotel worker thought for a moment. 'Mr. Spurgeon, if you are a smooth stone, I am only a pebble.'

That was not the direction Charles envisioned the conversation going, but he went with it. 'Ah,' he quickly replied, 'but you can build a church for God with pebbles just as high as you can with stones. What's your name, son?'

The hotel worker stretched out his hand. 'Francis.'

Charles shook it. 'How long have you worked at this hotel, Francis?'

'During the day I work here, but on the weekends I preach in a small church several miles (kilometres) away. We only have half a dozen members, but they love the Lord with all their heart. I am only eighteen years old and have never been formally trained as a preacher. Sometimes, I doubt if God is really being honoured by my sermons—they overspill with ignorance.'

Charles had been in those shoes before. 'Francis, I never went to college,' he said, 'and the Lord has supplied my every need. Every Christian is a student in the school of Christ,' Charles continued. 'We are always learning about the Saviour. Ironically, though I have no formal education, God has given me a school to train young men for the preaching ministry. We call it a pastors' college. We equip students just like you to go out into all the world and preach the good news of the Kingdom. Francis, how would you like to study theology and preaching in London?'

Francis didn't know what to say. To be able to return to his church with a better grasp of the Bible and how it applies to life would be greatly appreciated. 'It would be the greatest honour in my life,' the young man said.

'In 1874,' Charles said, 'we founded the college as an extension of our church's ministry. Every Friday, I lecture about preaching, theology, and sermon preparation. Now I have to be honest with you, Francis—the classes are demanding. You will be required to read exhaustively. Every week, you will have to preach a sermon in front of the whole class. They will critique your content, style, and delivery. Most students are intimidated to preach before their peers, but I have found the scrutiny to be helpful.'

Charles reached into his briefcase and pulled a paper from it. 'First, you must talk with God about this decision and see if He is leading you to London.'

Francis nodded. 'Thank you, Mr. Spurgeon. I will leave immediately and consult with God about the matter.'

Francis said goodbye and went back to the hotel. It was his break time, and he wanted to fill it with some serious praying.

Charles reached into his briefcase and removed a stack of unread letters. His goal for this vacation was to begin a commentary on the book of Matthew called *The Gospel of the Kingdom*. It was a daunting task that would require many hours, but since he was enjoying the beach so much, he decided to read his mail first. While he was away, Susannah always sent him his mail from London.

The first letter was familiar. It was the handwriting of his good friend. 'Ah, Mr. Moody,' Charles thought. 'What is God doing in your life these days?'

Charles held D. L. Moody in the highest esteem. He was a great evangelist in America, and his preaching drew thousands of sinners to Jesus Christ and the cross of salvation. Unfortunately, Charles had never had the opportunity to hear him preach in America, but in 1884, Moody came to London and preached in the Metropolitan Tabernacle for Charles' fiftieth birthday. It was a special moment for their friendship.

Moody was often called 'Crazy Moody' because he ministered to the poor people of Chicago. Everyone thought he was crazy because his compassion drove him to the poorest places. Often in tears, he would give them the gospel of hope, comfort, and love. His preaching was filled with fervour and his zeal stirred souls. Ever since Moody had met Spurgeon in 1867, the two had become immediate friends, and Charles always loved to exchange letters with him.

Charles read the latest letter.

Dear Charles,
It is with great joy that I write to you. For years I have thought more of you, than of any other man preaching

the gospel on this earth, and, to tell you the truth, I shrink from standing in your place. In comparison, I am unworthy even to blacken your boots. I have heard many preachers, but never have I seen the hand of God bless a spoken and written ministry as He has blessed yours. I admire your understanding of the Bible, your masterful sermons, and your compassion for the orphans of London. I must confess, however, that your prayers attract me most to your ministry. When you pray, I know you pull blessings down from above. As you are regaining your health in Mentone, may God give you the rest you need.

Yours truly,
D. L. Moody

Charles said a prayer for his friend and continued opening his letters.

Dear Mr. Spurgeon,
Many years ago, I met you on a London bench. You showed me undeserved kindness, compassion, and love. Thank you for allowing me to join your orphanage. Were it not for your intervention in my life, I might have died as a coughing chimney sweep. You changed my life and I am forever indebted to you.

I still have that boat you bought me – to this day, it still gives me hope. Jesus has become the captain of my heart and the ruler of my life.

I am now in my twenties and work full-time on a fishing boat. Thank you for being the father I never had.

Yours faithfully,
Edward Charles

The letter moved Charles to tears. He felt he had only enough emotions for one more letter. To his shock, it was from America:

Dear Rev. Spurgeon,

As you know, we wanted you to come to America for quite some time now. Your sermons are published weekly here, and it would be a great joy to have you lecture in our country.

Unfortunately, because you oppose slavery with such boldness and tenacity, your sermon sales in the South have decreased. People are refusing to buy your books. We think it would help your sales in our country, if you would come and speak to us in person.

All expenses would be covered for the journey, and you would be staying in the nicest hotels our country has. Please consider our invitation and write to us at your earliest convenience.

As long as you don't mention the issue of slavery ever again, all will be fine. We look forward to —

Charles stopped reading in the middle of the sentence. Frustration filled him. Pulling out a pen, his hand shook with eagerness to reply.

Dear Gentlemen,
Your invitation seems sincere; however, slavery is no small matter in my mind. If I came to America, I would speak against it as strongly as I have done before. It is an inhumane crime that draws no support or sympathy from me. Your country is but a child, acquiring the voice of a man. No doubt, God has His Holy hand on you

and I pray that He will bring you to full maturity soon. Unfortunately, my conscience on this issue is resolved, and since my health is deteriorating, such a trip would be unwise at this time. I will, however, continue to lift up your ministries in prayer, as you seek to spread the good news of Jesus Christ.
Truly yours,
C.H. Spurgeon

Charles sealed the envelope and sank back in his chair. He felt so passionately about this matter that relaxing had now become impossible. He walked up the beach and opened the door to the hotel.

'Mr. Spurgeon!' Francis said, grabbing Charles' briefcase. 'Let me carry this to your room.'

Charles agreed and followed Francis up the marble staircase. It was a spectacular hotel, filled with plants and mirrors. Charles understood why Queen Victoria stayed here. Charles' room was located on the second floor, a painful hike for an old man. It was worth it, though. Charles' windows opened to a beautiful view of the seascape.

Charles grabbed the railing, ascending the stairs. His knees began to throb. 'Here we go again!'

'Are you alright?' Francis asked, walking beside him.

Charles masked the pain. 'Oh, I'm well,' he said. 'It's just my joints. They sometimes give me problems. But when I was your age I could —'

Charles slipped. Francis reached out to grab him, but Charles fell head first down the staircase, completing two full somersaults. Francis gasped in horror as Charles landed face first on the marble floor.

'Somebody help!' Francis yelled, rushing down the stairs. Charles lay on his stomach, unconscious and bleeding. People rushed to his aid.

'He's dead!' one lady yelled. Blood gushed from Spurgeon's lip.

Francis rolled Charles onto his back. 'We need a doctor! Get a doctor here now!'

Francis put his ear to Charles' mouth. 'He's still breathing!'

Charles began to shake. 'He's going into shock!' Francis held Charles' shoulders firmly to the ground. 'Mr. Spurgeon, can you hear me?'

Charles' mouth slowly moved.

'He's trying to talk,' an old lady said.

Francis listened. A faint noise could be detected, but it was too soft to decipher. 'What are you trying to say?'

'Shhhhh! Everyone be quiet!' yelled the woman. 'He's saying his dying wish.'

The noise from Spurgeon's lips grew more audible. Soon, everyone recognized it. Charles was laughing. Louder and louder he laughed, until everyone standing above his trembling body joined him in laughter. They helped him to his feet. His back ached, his joints burned, but Charles had suffered no serious harm.

'Just a couple of bruises and a bloody mouth,' Charles mumbled. 'That's all.'

'We thought you were dead!' Francis cried.

Charles chuckled. 'God must still have work for me to do on this earth.' He pulled a blue, polka-dotted handkerchief from his pocket and wiped the blood from his mouth. 'At last, this old hand cloth has fulfilled a noble purpose.'

'That was quite a fall,' Francis said, relieved that Charles was not dead.

The elderly woman bent over. She saw something shiny lying on the ground. 'What's this?' she asked, examining the white object. Suddenly, her legs gave way beneath her and she collapsed in a terrifying faint.

'My tooth!' Charles shrieked, licking his gums. Finally, the doctor arrived on the scene.

'Which one of you needs the most medical attention?' he asked, looking at the collapsed woman and the bleeding preacher.

Charles pointed to the woman. 'Help her.'

'But he just fell down the stairs,' Francis said, pointing at Charles.

'Yes, but the whole ordeal was really just painless dentistry,' he said, maintaining his sense of humour. 'That tooth was bothering me, anyway.'

Everyone laughed.

Charles needed to lie down. 'I'll try the staircase one more time. Perhaps the second time will be safer than the first,' he thought. As he hugged the railing, four people carefully followed him.

'Just in case you fall ...' Francis said, ready to catch him this time.

Francis walked with Charles down the hallway and placed his briefcase by the door of his room.

'Thank you, Francis,' Charles said, handing him money for his services.

'I cannot accept that,' he said. 'You have already given me more than I ever could have imagined. Your words to me on the beach were treasure enough.'

Charles said goodbye and opened the door to his room. It was time for a well-deserved nap. Reaching into his briefcase, he pulled out the last letter he had not yet read. It was from Susannah.

Sweet Charles,

I have missed you terribly! May God give you rest and relaxation. You certainly need it — your responsibilities would overwhelm anyone in your position. You are a pastor, writer, lecturer, dean of the Pastors' College, and administrator of an orphanage. I wish I could be with you now to comfort and hold you in my arms.

It is foggy here in London, but it gives me great joy to know that the air is clearer for you in France. May the weather bring healing to your body and peace to your soul.

The book fund has increased. Ever since we started it fourteen years ago, it has blessed many pastors across this country. I receive weekly letters of thanksgiving for the books we provide to the Christian ministers who cannot afford to pay the regular price for them.

Also, there have been many generous contributions to the Pastors' Aid Foundation. Several pastors in our city are struggling to feed their families and have asked me to thank you for this ministry. Last week, we gave them food, clothes, and medicine. They are so grateful.

Our sons are doing well. Thomas has expressed interest in being an artist and a preacher. He is following in his father's footsteps. Charles has been writing some of his own sermons, too.

We all miss you very much.

Love always,
Susannah

Charles put down the letter and walked to the window, thankful, at peace, and longing to be home.

Grace for Gout

Mr. and Mrs. Charles Spurgeon's home, Westwood, London – 1891

'It's rheumatic gout,' Dr. Miller whispered in Susannah's ear. 'And it has affected his entire body.'

Susannah trembled. 'This disease has plagued him for so long,' she said. 'He says it feels like the bite of a cobra, injecting venom into his veins. It has become the main source of his depression.' She placed a wet towel on her husband's forehead.

'I need to ask you some questions about Mr. Spurgeon,' Dr. Miller said.

'Absolutely, anything.'

'How long has he been sleeping in bed?'

Susannah looked at Charles. 'Two days now – I'm very worried about him. He's never been this ill before. Do you have any idea what is causing his sickness?'

Dr. Miller had an idea, but it was not grounded in medical experience. 'Personally, I think this sickness is Satan's last attempt to halt your husband's ministry.' Dr. Miller looked into her eyes. 'This might be a blizzard we will not be able to escape.'

Susannah shuddered. 'No, God, please don't take him away!'

'Some people think gout is related to diet. Has Charles ever considered becoming a vegetarian?'

'Well, actually, yes.' she said. 'Several years ago he avoided meat like it was the plague. He lost eight inches off his stomach! It was the healthiest I have seen him since we stood together at the marriage altar.' She smiled. 'But that was short-lived—he insisted meat was too precious to give up. He says that God gave us teeth for a reason, and he was surely going to put his to good use. Charles now eats lamb, beef, quail, and every animal he can sink his teeth into.'

Dr. Miller was concerned. 'How much does he exercise?'

Susannah chuckled at the thought of her husband exercising. 'He loves long walks, if that counts.'

Dr. Miller raised his eyebrows. 'Is he involved in a sport of any kind?'

'Charles was never involved in sports. He exercises his brain more than his body. In fact, he even told me that while he was preaching, he counted up to eight thoughts happening simultaneously in his mind. Even if he wanted to exercise, his busy schedule would not permit it.'

'I know Mr. Spurgeon is a very busy man,' Dr. Miller said, 'but he will be far more effective in his ministry if he adopts a better diet and begins exercising regularly. Do you know of any other habits that might be contributing to his failing health?'

Charles Spurgeon

Susannah could think of one more. 'He smokes cigars like a chimney!' she said. 'But that does not hurt his health, does it, doctor?'

'Well, actually, it's controversial, but there are new theories in the medical community that lead us to believe that smoking might be toxic to the lungs. Since your husband uses his lungs so much behind the pulpit, it might be best for him to quit smoking.'

Susannah never liked the smell of cigar smoke. 'He always told me it helped relax his throat before he preached—a stress relief.'

Dr. Miller knew several tobacco-smoking patients who died prematurely. He was convinced their deaths were related to the habit. 'How does your husband deal with pressure?'

'At best, poorly,' she said. 'The weight of the world lies heavily on his shoulders. Sometimes, he sinks so deeply into depression, that I fear his sanity will snap.'

'Give me an example of one of the pressures in his life,' Dr. Miller said.

There were many. 'Well,' Susannah said, 'Ever since Charles Darwin's book, *On the Origin of Species*, was published in 1859, Charles has spent a lot of energy combating its theory. Throughout all of England, Darwin's book has become influential. My husband utterly rejects the theory of evolution – the idea that the world evolved from nothing with no design or purpose. Charles thinks it's silly to believe that we evolved from primates. He thinks it's sillier that churches are being sympathetic to the concept.'

'What are some other stresses in his life?'

Susannah could list dozens. 'Are you familiar with the Down Grade Controversy?'

'No.'

'It all started when the New Theology movement swept through our country. Charles is also vocal about this movement. The heart of the problem is this: modern rationalists are seeking to understand the Bible purely from a scientific perspective. They discredit any elements of Christianity that do not make sense to them. They view the Holy Bible as an historical compilation of fairy tales – void of any inspiration of the Holy Spirit. Anything they cannot replicate in the science lab and pass through the scientific method, they dismiss as irrational – the virgin birth of Jesus, the miracles, the resurrection, etc. Charles fights against this heresy and will not budge on the matter. In his book *The Sword and the Trowel,* Charles said that the new theology is really just old heresy, putting the church on a down grade. Ever since, it has become known as the Down Grade Controversy.'

'From what you have told me,' Dr. Miller said, 'Charles has too many stresses in his life. He needs more rest.' Placing his hands on Charles, Dr. Miller prayed for a quick recovery. After he finished, he gathered up his medical equipment and walked to the door.

'Thank you so much for coming on such short notice, doctor.'

Dr. Miller turned around. 'Call me if Charles is still sleeping in the morning. My prayers are with you both.'

Susannah closed the door behind him and went back into Charles' room. 'My sweet Charles,' she said, squeezing his hand. 'God, comfort my husband while he sleeps,' she prayed. 'Does he still have work to do for you on this earth? Are there no more sermons to preach or souls to save? Has the well of his ministry run dry? Oh God, is there no more grace for his gout?' Susannah could not look at him any longer. His face was too quiet – too deathly. Night was fast approaching, and she decided to finish editing his sermon.

Sitting in a comfortable chair in Charles' study, she went to work. This was her passion, her greatest honour. Ever since their marriage, Susannah had edited his work. She knew how fast his thoughts sometimes flowed. He did not need to be worried about punctuation in those moments; he just needed to get the thoughts out. Susannah could polish them for publication later.

She twisted the knob on the side of the lantern, extending the wick. The flame burned brighter.

On average, Charles wrote five hundred letters a week with his own hand. It was an enormous task. His recent sickness prevented such work, and Susannah picked up where he left off. Every week she mailed Charles' sermons all over the world. There was a huge demand for his words. Some preachers used his sermons on Sunday morning instead of their own – a practice Charles never agreed with. Dozens of countries received his weekly homily: Australia, Jamaica, and parts of Africa amongst them. Susannah loved this ministry – it was her ministry to her husband, and she worked at it with all her heart.

Susannah picked up Charles' latest sermon. She began to read it:

'There must be a revival of the old gospel preaching. We must have it back. Our ministers must return to the same gospel which John Bunyan and George Whitefield preached – a biblical gospel. We cannot embrace these new philosophical gospels that do not believe in the miracles of the Bible or the power of the resurrection. We must bring them together – these false gospels, these geological gospels – and do with them as the people of Ephesus did with the evil books – we must burn them and hear the preaching of Paul once again. We can do without the theory of evolution, but we cannot do without the ancient gospel. We can do without fancy speeches and fine eloquence, but we cannot do without Christ, and Christ crucified. Lord, revive thy work in your world by giving us the old-fashioned gospel back in our pulpits.'

Thirty years of marriage had almost been a blur to Susannah. The burning attraction she felt for him was far from fizzling out. He had turned out just the way she thought he would – his hopes and dreams had come true. His ambition was just as strong, his conviction just as deep. He was her warrior, courageously standing up for the Bible, defeating the powers of darkness with the gospel of light. Her prayers for his recovery were as potent as ever, and above all, she wanted an end to his miserable suffering.

Knock. Knock. Knock. 'Who could that be at this hour?' Susannah wondered. She put down the sermon and opened the front door.

'Good evening, mother.'

'Thomas! What a surprise.' She hugged and kissed him. He looked tired and miserable. 'Are you alright?' she asked.

'Yes, but I need to talk with you about something.'

'Come in, your father is resting, but we can talk in the study.' Thomas followed her inside.

'Lila and I have been married for three years now,' he said. 'I need some advice.' Thomas knew he could trust his mother's advice. She had experienced the ups and downs of marriage and was like a well of wisdom when it came to love, romance, and relationships.

Thomas sat down next to her. 'Lila has been the greatest wife I could have ever hoped to marry, but recently we have been arguing a lot. We quarrel about the small stuff—the unimportant stuff. Is that normal?'

Susannah knew exactly what Thomas was going through. She and Charles had their rough moments during the first three years of their marriage. 'There are times,' she said, 'when love is easy. It is not a problem to love someone when life is smooth. But let me tell you a secret ...'

Thomas listened. He needed all the secrets he could get.

'Love is not always a feeling,' she continued. 'Love is a commitment. Your father and I have been committed to one another for many long years. We have seen fortune and famine together. Now, there have been times when we radically disagreed, but I discovered in those difficult moments what love is really about – friendship. Friends stick together no matter what.'

Thomas was curious. 'When were you the most frustrated with him?'

Susannah smiled, nostalgically. 'Let me tell you a story. It was shortly before our wedding day and Charles was scheduled to preach to a large crowd in London. I wanted to hear him and offer my support on that special occasion, so I planned to go with him. All week I counted down the days until we left. Finally, when we arrived at the church, Charles did the unthinkable – the unimaginable. Do you know what he did?'

Thomas could only imagine.

'Charles completely forgot I was there! He was so caught up in the preaching moment, that he walked off and left me before he went to the pulpit to preach.

I was at the mercy of the crowds, fending for myself, almost trampled by the multitudes.'

Thomas laughed at the mistake.

'I fumed with anger! Never had I envisioned a man treating me with such disrespect and neglect! I was born a Victorian lady – honoured and cherished. I felt so abandoned, neglected, and insignificant that I stormed out of the event, while Charles was in the middle of his sermon. I walked all the way home. After the sermon, he must have realized his costly error and came looking for me. I was weeping in my room when he reached my home. My mother explained to him the importance of relational responsibility. He was very apologetic. I have never seen him so sorry for anything. I forgave him and we were reconciled. After that incident, however, Charles asked me to edit every one of his sermons before he preached them. He wanted me to be, forever, included in that intimate part of his life.'

Susannah pointed to the sermon she was editing. 'To this day, I have not stopped.'

Thomas felt reassured. 'So, conflict is a normal part of a relationship?'

'Not only is it normal, Thomas, it should be expected. How you handle your conflicts will determine the strength of your friendship. Never let the sun go down on your anger, my son.'

Thomas nodded in agreement, grateful for the advice. He stopped thinking about his marriage and thought about hers instead. 'How is Father doing, anyway?' he asked. 'What did the doctor say?'

'He's not doing any better, but it's too early to tell. The doctor said his fever is too high and he needs to quit smoking and become a vegetarian.'

'I can't see Dad doing any one of those things,' he said.

'Your father is a unique man. God broke the mould when he made Charles. He is like a diamond. The gospel shines through his life in a spectacular way. He is multifaceted, but like most diamonds, he is not without a flaw or two.'

Thomas lowered his voice. 'There's a rumour spreading around the church. They say he's going to die soon.'

Susannah wanted to end that rumour quickly. 'God decides when a person is ready to die,' she sharply replied. 'Your father has lived through many painful trials. Every one of them has contributed to his wisdom and spiritual insight. I am confident he will wake up tomorrow, stronger than ever.' She convinced herself of this.

'He's only fifty-seven-years-old,' Thomas said. 'but the grey hair and the lines of his face make him look much older. He looks like my grandfather, not my father.

Susannah loved his lines. 'There is more experience in those lines than most men collect in two lifetimes,' she said. 'He has certainly earned those lines. He writes four books a year and has preached to ten million people over the span of his lifetime. God has used your father in mighty ways and history will have to wait a long time before it ever sees lines like those again.' Susannah was proud of her husband.

Thomas knew his mother needed to be alone. 'He will get better,' he said, encouraging her. 'God is not done with him yet.' After hugging his mother, Thomas showed himself to the door.

Susannah edited Charles' sermon for twenty more minutes, but his words brought back too many memories. Her heart could take no more and she drifted to sleep in the chair.

Suddenly, she was looking into Charles' young, hazel eyes. They were innocent and inexperienced, unprepared for the many miseries they would later see. She ran her hands through his dark hair as his baritone voice echoed in her ears. It was a voice that could change the world. She was nervous again. How fiercely her heart did beat for him! And suddenly he's on his knee, asking to spend the rest of his life with her. It felt like yesterday; the tears were still salty on her lips. They were twenty, and it was yesterday – a yesterday she wanted to keep forever.

'Susannah,' she whispered to herself, 'Open your eyes.' Susannah woke abruptly in the chair. The study was empty. 'Just a dream.'

Walking into the kitchen, she began to boil a pot of water. Twice a day she did this for Charles. He was fast asleep, but she knew the warmth of the cloth brought him comfort. On Sunday mornings, before he preached, she would prepare a cup of vinegar for his voice. He sipped it, while she put the boiled washcloth on his brow. Often, she would walk into his study to find him lying face first to the floor, deep in depression. He felt so unworthy to be preaching the Word of God. He was a man who took preaching seriously. It often drove him to despair. He felt so responsible for the souls God had entrusted to him, and if Susannah could help him by boiling washcloths and brewing vinegar, she would certainly do it. She believed it would help him get better. She had to believe.

Susannah opened the door to his bedroom. 'Charles?'

No reply.

His bed was empty. 'Charles?' she shouted.

Bed sheets covered the floor. 'Perhaps he is in the study.' She walked into the study in search of him. The glass doors leading out to the balcony were open.

As she ventured into the darkness, she saw the silhouette of her husband leaning on the railing. She traced the figure with her eyes. 'Charles? Are you alright?'

No response.

Susannah went to him. Sweat covered his body. He was shaking from head to heel.

'What are you doing out here?'

He looked at her.

'Susie?'

He wasn't acting like himself. Charles never stood so close to the railing – he hated heights. She grabbed his arm and tried to pull him inside.

'Come inside, dear husband. You will take a chill out here.'

He resisted her efforts.

'Do you hear that?' he asked.

Susannah did not want to hear anything; she only wanted her husband to come inside where it was safe, where it was warm.

'Listen,' Charles said, hushing her.

She listened.

'I think they're singing,' he said.

'My husband is delusional,' she thought. But then she heard it too. It sounded like a choir of crickets singing in the distance.

Charles was captivated by the noise. 'Even in the blackest of nights,' he said, 'God's creatures sing their praises to Him.'

Susannah saw the sermon in the making and knew her husband was about to say something brilliant.

'And if little crickets can praise God in the dark,' he continued, 'how much more should humans do the same?'

Susannah understood.

'I may have gout, sweet Susie, but God's grace is sufficient for my sickness, and I will love Him, praise

Him, and thank Him until the moment He takes me from this world.' He kissed her cheek – it was wet with tears.

Charles held her closely to his chest. 'Before I die, there is one more thing I must do …'

Charles looked into her eyes. 'I must preach Jesus one more time.'

The Queen Arrives

London, England – Sunday morning,
(one month later) 7th June, 1891

A horse-drawn carriage raced through the narrow, cobblestone streets of London. As a storm gathered outside, Queen Victoria's eyes flared with wild determination.

'We must turn back,' Alice begged, holding onto her seat for dear life. 'It's too dangerous to go on!'

'We will continue,' the Queen said, tapping her fists against the ceiling of the carriage. 'Faster! Faster! We must make it to the Tabernacle!'

The carriage driver thrashed the panting horses harder with the reins.

'Why must we hear him today?' Alice asked. 'There are safer Sundays to hear him preach – sunny Sundays without wind, rain, and horrible weather.'

Victoria grew impatient. 'Charles Haddon Spurgeon is preaching his last sermon this morning,' she said. 'Nothing in heaven above or earth below will keep me from hearing it – not you, not this flimsy carriage, and especially not this thunderstorm!'

The Prince of Preachers

'But, your Majesty,' Alice cried, looking out the window, 'we are going too fast! These roads are too slippery!'

The carriage cut into the foggy darkness, nearly missing benches, buildings, and bridges. 'We are risking our very lives to hear this preacher!' Alice whimpered.

Victoria paused. 'When you are older,' she said, 'you will learn what I have learned this morning …'

Alice tilted her head with intrigue.

'Some things,' she said, 'are worth risking life for. We are not far from the Metropolitan Tabernacle,' she said. 'It would be foolish to turn back now.'

Alice couldn't complain. 'Yes, your Majesty,' she mumbled, following the Queen out of the carriage and down the foggy road. 'Spurgeon better be the greatest preacher in the whole world,' she thought.

The tabernacle was taller than they expected. Six massive columns supported the front of the church. Floods of people pushed to get inside. Victoria pulled her hood over her head. Her cheeks were still dark with ashes. 'For the first time in my life,' she thought, 'I don't look like a Queen.'

A group of rowdy boys rushed past, bumping into the disguised queen. Victoria lost her balance.

'Your Majesty!' Alice yelled, reaching for the Queen. People glanced at them curiously.

'Shhhh!' Victoria whispered, standing up. 'Don't call me that in public!'

The interior of the Metropolitan Tabernacle was breathtaking. Thousands of people swarmed to their seats, like bees buzzing inside a honeycomb. The skeleton of the sanctuary was cylindrical. It contained two sets of balconies lining the upper floors.

'Where shall we sit?' Alice asked, looking for empty pews.

There was an empty section four rows from the front, but Victoria was hesitant about walking down the centre aisle – someone might recognize her. If newspapers discovered that the Queen of England had sneaked out of the palace to hear a preacher that the newspapers already hated, it might completely ruin her popularity. Nevertheless, she had confidence in her dirty disguise, and she wanted to be as close to Spurgeon as possible. She walked down the aisle.

Sinking in their seats, Alice and Victoria were glad to be sitting on something that didn't move, shake, break, or crash. Wooden pews had never felt so secure.

Henry and his wife, Mary, sat down in a pew near the back of the sanctuary. 'After all these years,' Mary said, 'Charles is preaching his final sermon. The first time I saw him, he was just a poor teenager trying to get an interview with a college principal.'

Henry chuckled. 'And you showed him into the wrong room.'

'It was meant to be,' she replied, smiling.

'I've known Charles longer than anyone here,' Henry said. 'We were once boys, wrestling in the grassy fields of Cambridge. Charles was never good at sports, and to this day he can't block a punch. But those things don't matter. Charles breathes the Bible. Make no mistake, Mary; he is like a tree planted by streams of water.'

Mary liked the thought. 'Now his branches extend all the way around the world. What do you think his text will be for this morning?'

'Whatever it is,' Henry said, 'Jesus Christ will be the theme. Charles finds Him on every page of the Bible.'

Mary could believe it. She had heard Charles preach when she attended his church in Waterbeach. They had taught her the basics of reading and writing. Charles always reminded her that every word in the Bible, both in the Old and New Testament, in some way points to Jesus.

'It seems appropriate,' Mary said, 'for you to hear his last sermon. Forty years ago, you were with him for his first. Tell me about that night again.'

Henry had told her that story a hundred times, but somehow it never grew old.

'Well, it all started when Charles found out he was going to be the preacher for the evening in Teversham.'

A group of deacons entered the sanctuary. They sat in the pews in front of Queen Victoria and Alice. Susannah was the last to take her seat. It was a sad morning for her. She had known this day would come. Her husband's health was ebbing. His gout was getting worse. A wife can handle only so much pain, and the sound of his agonies in the night quickly crossed the threshold of her tolerance. The moon that brightly shone in London was waning. The tree that towered over England was falling. And her heart was heavy.

The Metropolitan Tabernacle was filled to capacity. Those who were not fortunate enough to find seats in the pews gladly stood in the aisles. People pressed against one another, shoulder to shoulder, awaiting the sight of Spurgeon.

Charles sat in the pastor's study. He had sat here many times before, meeting with God before he would dare to preach His Word. He loved the smell of the books around him. He liked to surround himself with the thoughts of those who had preached in the past. He felt connected to them. Their message of salvation was his own message. Their passion for proclaiming the sovereignty of the Saviour was his passion. Their struggles with the world, the flesh, and the devil were his struggles, too. 'Perhaps in the future, some boy or girl will be searching through a dusty attic and will come across one of my books. Perhaps God will use my words to shape and mould the hearts and lives of future Christians.'

Charles reviewed his sermon notes. It was only an outline – he had stopped writing out his sermons word for word many years ago. He didn't like being stuck to the sentences any more than a lion liked being caged in a zoo. Charles needed room to roam and roar.

'I am an old man, now, Lord,' he prayed. 'My hair is grey, my legs are weak, and my eyes are dull. But you are the God who gives us exactly what we need when we need it. You gave Samson the strength to kill a thousand enemies at the end of his life. Give me the opposite at the end of mine. Let your Word go out of my mouth and save thousands of lost souls. Let me decrease for the last time while You increase.'

Knock. Knock. Knock.

'Come in,' Charles said.

A deacon entered. It was John Harrald, a man who had known Charles from the very beginning of his ministry in London. 'It is time,' he said.

Charles knew it was time. He knew this was the last time he would stand before his congregation. Charles knew. But knowing did not stop the hurting.

'Thank you,' he said.

John smiled. 'For what?'

Charles looked at him. 'For always knocking.'

The two men walked down the hall towards the sanctuary. They had done this a thousand times over the years.

'When the time comes,' Charles said, 'remember, a plain stone. C.H. Spurgeon – nothing more. I don't want much fuss to be made about my funeral.'

John nodded and opened the sanctuary door for him. A wave of silence swept the crowd. Everyone strained their eyes to see the preacher. For many, this was their first time to visit the tabernacle. Suddenly, their anticipation was over and an old, heavy-set man emerged on the platform. His steps were slow and aided by a black, wooden cane.

'At last,' Queen Victoria said, 'Charles Haddon Spurgeon – we shall finally hear the greatest preacher of our time.' She set her eyes on Charles and looked at him as though he were a king. 'So, this is the man everyone is talking about.'

Alice examined him, too. He was shorter than she expected. His blue suit clung snugly around his body. A blue, polka-dotted handkerchief poked out of his pocket. And yet there was a tenderness about him.

Charles surveyed the crowds. These were his favourite people in all the world. His joints burned with gout, his ankles throbbed with pain, and his head swirled with dizziness. But no matter how hard he tried, he could not keep the smile from his face. It was good for Charles to be in the house of the Lord one more time.

Susannah saw the twinkle in his eye. She knew he was suffering in the flesh, but in the spirit, he was as vibrant as ever. This was the pinnacle of his preaching ministry, and he had not left his joyful heart at home.

It was time to begin. As Charles opened his mouth to pray, he felt fatigued and had difficulty opening his mouth. 'Why am I struggling with words?' he wondered. He grasped the railing.

Henry watched in horror. 'He's not going to make it!'

Susannah shut her eyes. He was going to fall.

Suddenly, Charles was back in Teversham. It was the evening of his first sermon. He saw the faces of the farmers; he heard the whispers of their wives. Children giggled in the corner. It was all coming back to him—the barren kitchen, the Cambridge paintings, the leaky, thatched roof. Charles took a deep breath. He was not in a city cathedral; he was in a simple cottage. Surely he could tell a bunch of farmers about the love of Jesus. Surely he could point them to the cross. And Charles regained his strength, stood, and opened his mouth to pray.

Heads bowed and eyes closed as Charles presented his plea before the Maker of heaven and earth. With simple language, he spoke to God. His voice was friendly and comfortable, as if he had known God a long time. His words were powerful and piercing, arresting the attention of the Almighty.

And then the sermon.

'Dear soul,' he began, 'be content wherever God has put you. Do not think that only preachers, missionaries, and Bible teachers can glorify God. God is glorified by people of all positions – the poor carpenter praising Jesus in his woodshed, the chimney sweep begging God to wash him white as snow, the simple servant girl singing her songs to the Saviour. Let us think little of ourselves, dear congregation, but let never think little of our callings.'

Victoria was moved to memory. 'I have never once thought little of myself.'

Charles continued. 'It was a cold morning in January. I was only fifteen years old. I burned with the flames of guilt. I didn't know much, but I did know that I was a sinner and I had to find an answer.

'I trudged through a blizzard to find relief. I should have died in the snow, but somehow I ended up in a small church on Artillery Street. And I can still hear them singing – so loud and powerful – like angels.

'The pastor had been snowed in and an old, uneducated shoemaker climbed into the pulpit. His words were blunt. His thoughts were plain. He lacked eloquence. But his message was meaty. He told me to look to Jesus and I would be saved. Forty-one years later, I am still looking at the Saviour. If God can use a simple shoemaker to convert a young, rough child, he can use you—no matter how rich, smart, or talented you are. Simple people make great soul winners.' Charles scanned the sanctuary.

'Maybe you are sitting here and you are looking for God in all the wrong places. You think He's in money, but you can never get enough of it. You think He's in popularity, but someone more important than you shows up. Where can you look to find the Saviour? Look to the cross, dear soul and be ye saved. God offers you His life, He offers you His love, and He offers you His everlasting atonement. If you take a step towards Him today, you will find that God's already taken a thousand steps towards you.'

Alice listened to his words. 'How can I love someone I have never seen, heard, or touched?'

Charles continued. 'Jesus Christ is a marvellous magnet, drawing us to Himself. I have heard that when builders want to build a bridge over a great chasm, they shoot across the river, an arrow or a bullet that draws a tiny piece of thread. By means of that little thread, they draw across a piece of twine, and when they grasp it on the other side, they bind a small rope to the end of the twine. Then to that rope they tie a cable, and from that cable, they attach pieces of iron. This is the way they build the bridge.

'This is also how Jesus unites Himself with us. He may give us only a thread of thought, but He then gives a sense of pleasant interest, and then some deeper feeling, then a crushing emotion, then a faint faith, then a stronger faith, until at last we have become firmly bound to Christ.' Charles looked down at Alice. 'So be thankful if you only have a thread of communication between you and Jesus. It will certainly lead to more.'

Charles looked at Susannah. 'There will be a day when every tear will be wiped from every eye; every sickness will be wiped from every saint. A day is coming when we shall meet our Maker face to face, embracing Him with arms outstretched. When that day arrives for me, do not be overcome with sadness.'

Susannah nodded.

'For the Christian, death is the sweetest part of life.' Spurgeon continued. 'Every caterpillar must travel through a cocoon before riding the wings of the wind.'

Charles looked at Mary, Henry's wife. 'Never forget that you are pilgrims in this world. You are on a journey to Jesus. Keep your eyes on the prize. And when you walk through the valley of the shadow of death, remember that is only a shadow – and you serve the God of all light.'

Finally, Charles glanced at the Queen. His eyes seemed to stare right through her – through the ash, through the cloak, right into her very soul. 'Perhaps you have come to church this morning and you are at the end of your rope. On the outside, you are one way, but on the inside you are searching for God. Is your hope gone? Is your health gone? Are your friends gone? Are your dreams gone? Is your faith dry? Is your love scarce? Is your peace passed? Has your grief grown? Has your pain peaked? Have your tears triumphed? Then look to Jesus!' Charles said. 'Look to Him with all your might! There is enough salvation for you in just one look! Look and live, look and live!'

It was time to pray. Charles bowed his head. Before he closed his eyes he cast his eyes around the congregation. Young men and women who had grown up through the church and Sunday school. Fellow pastors and preachers who had been helped through Spurgeon's own writings and charity. Men and women from the city and the country. Rich and poor. Tall and short. Old and young.

In one corner, there was a lad like so many of the young lads before him – an ex-Stockwell orphanage boy, most likely. 'Edward?' Charles asked himself. Perhaps.

Across the aisle, Charles smiled at the image of an old man in a corner pew staring back at him. The clothes and the rough country garb spoke of a tradesman. 'He could even be a shoemaker,' Charles thought to himself.

And with that thought, Charles found himself looking at his life in one long glance. He smelt the hot tea brewing on his mother's stove. He felt the sting of the snow in the Colchester ice storm. He heard another shoemaker's voice screaming through the darkness. He watched the balcony collapse at the Surrey Music Hall. He tasted Susannah's sweet kiss on their wedding day. He buried his toes in the cool Mentone sand.

And now, standing before his congregation at the very end of his life, he knew that he was on the verge of meeting his Saviour. After half a century of living, Charles eagerly awaited that.

The congregation poured out of the sanctuary: shoemakers, laundry maids, shop owners and more important people of state ... they had all come to hear Charles Haddon Spurgeon preach his very last sermon.

And as the very last people disappeared, two women remained quietly in the pew. Is it possible that the Queen of England was taught by the Prince of Preachers how to love the King of Heaven?

Author's Note

On 1st January, 1892, in Mentone, France, Charles Haddon Spurgeon blinked his last. In the final moments of his life, Susannah was at his side. She heard the last words from his lips: 'Oh wifey, I have had such a blessed time with my Lord. My work is done. I have fought the good fight. I have finished my course. I have kept the faith.'

At five minutes past eleven, the pilgrim went home. A telegraph was sent around the world, spreading the news of his death. Everyone from Asia to Australia to America mourned his loss. The nineteenth century might have lost one of its greatest preachers – a man of whom the world was not worthy – but heaven gained one of its greatest saints.

Now, did the Queen of England listen to the Prince of Preachers? It may be one of those stories that has just travelled down the corridor of time. There is no record. There is no 'real' evidence … but often truth is stranger than fiction. The real story of this book is the fact that Charles Spurgeon loved the King of kings. Whether you were prince or pauper, Queen of England or the beggar within the sound of Bow Bells, he would tell you about his Lord and Saviour, Jesus Christ. There are two names that you should focus on in this tale – Charles Spurgeon, Prince of Preachers and Jesus Christ, King of Kings and Lord of Lords.

Charles Spurgeon Timeline

1830	French Revolution.
1831	Faraday demonstrates electromagnetic induction.
1834	Charles Spurgeon born.
1837	Queen Victoria ascends the throne.
1839	Bicycle invented.
1843	Dickens' *A Christmas Carol* published.
1844	Dumas' *The Three Musketeers* published.
1850	Spurgeon converted.
1851	Spurgeon preaches first sermon.
1852	Spurgeon becomes pastor of Baptist church at Waterbeach, Cambridgeshire.
1854	Spurgeon becomes pastor of New Park Street Church.
1855	David Livingstone finds the Victoria Falls.
1856	Spurgeon marries Susannah Thompson. Surrey Gardens Music Hall tragedy.
1857	The Pastors' College opens (renamed Spurgeon's College in 1923). *The Saint and His Saviour* published.
1859	First American oil well drilled in Pennsylvania.
1861	Spurgeon's congregation moves to Metropolitan Tabernacle. American Civil War begins.

1863	Football Association founded.
	Battle of Gettysburg.
1864	Red Cross established.
1866	Colportage Association founded to provide affordable Christian literature.
	Morning by Morning published.
1867	The Stockwell Orphanage for boys opens (Girls' orphanage opens in 1879).
	U.S.A. buys Alaska from Russia.
1868	*Evening by Evening* published.
1869	*John Ploughman's Talk* published.
1876	Victoria proclaimed Empress of India.
1885	Mark Twain's *Huckleberry Finn* published.
1887	Spurgeon leaves the Baptist Union.
1888	Van Gogh paints *Sunflowers*.
1891	First telephone link between London and Paris.
1892	Charles Spurgeon dies.

Charles Spurgeon: Life Summary

Born in Kelvedon, Essex, Spurgeon's conversion to Christianity came in 1850 at the age of fifteen. During a snow storm, he was forced into a small Methodist chapel in Colchester where Spurgeon said, himself, 'God opened my heart to the salvation message.'

He preached his first sermon in 1851 and became known as an able and popular preacher of God's Word.

In 1852, he became pastor of a church at Waterbeach, Cambridgeshire, and in 1854, at twenty years of age, Spurgeon was called to the pastorate of London's New Park Street Chapel, Southwark.

Spurgeon was a Baptist and a Calvinist and often preached to audiences of more than 10,000. The congregation quickly outgrew their building and moved to Surrey Music Hall. In 1861, they moved permanently to the Metropolitan Tabernacle at Elephant and Castle, seating five thousand people with standing room for another thousand.

By the time of his death in 1892, he had preached almost thirty-six hundred sermons and published forty-nine volumes of commentaries, sayings, anecdotes, illustrations, and devotions.

In 1856, Spurgeon married Susannah, daughter of Robert Thompson of Falcon Square, London, by whom he had twin sons, Charles and Thomas. He suffered ill health towards the end of his life, suffering from rheumatism, gout, and Bright's disease. He would often retreat to Mentone, near Nice, France, to recuperate. It was there, that he eventually died in 1892.

Thinking Further Topics

1. The Queen of England in Disguise

I'm sure you've often wondered what you would do if you were a king or queen. The author here has imagined what it would be like for Queen Victoria, if she had wanted to be 'normal' like everyone else – just for a day. Everyone else, at that time, was going to hear Charles Spurgeon preach. She probably wanted to as well. In fact she may very well have. There is a strong rumour that she did attend at least one of his services, but there is no absolute proof that she did. However, he was an important preacher of his day. It would have been quite in order for the Queen of England to hear the Prince of Preachers.

But let's think about the Prince of Peace – Jesus Christ. That's who Spurgeon preached about.

Jesus knows you inside out. He knows your plans and dreams and thoughts. Study God's Word and find out His plans for you.

'For I know the plans I have for you,' declares the Lord. 'Plans to prosper you and not to harm you, plans to give you hope and a future.'
(Jeremiah 29:11 NIV)

2. A Burning Sermon on a Snowy Sunday

Imagine you have just fallen over the edge of a dangerous cliff. You are on some rocks and the only way to safety is if you cling onto a rope that is being offered to you by a rescuer. The rescuer is on the cliff above and he is calling down to you, 'Look here! I'm here!' But you refuse to look and so you miss the rope. Instead you sit and look at the sea gulls overhead. What help are they? Nothing! It is the one with the rope you should look to.

Jesus is the one with the rope here. He is the one who will save you from sin and eternal death. He has salvation purchased for sinners on the cross at Calvary.

Charles Spurgeon was told to look to Jesus and be saved. You are being told this too!

'Look unto me, and be ye saved, all the ends of the earth, for I am God, and there is none else.'
(Isaiah 45:22)

3. Preaching to the Poor

God gave Spurgeon a special gift – the gift of preaching. Charles began to use that from an early age. Think about your gifts and abilities. What has God given to you?

Your mind, your body, your energy are just three. What about your time, your hobbies, your character, friends and family? The list is endless.

Give thanks to God for all the good things He has given to you and use these things in your life to honour Him.

'Every good and perfect gift is from above, coming down from the Father of the heavenly lights, who does not change like shifting shadows.'
(James 1:17 NIV)

4. A Pilgrim's Progress

The Pilgrim's Progress was one of Spurgeon's favourite books. It was an allegory of the Christian life. Christian, the main character in the book, had to walk to the Celestial City. It was a hard and difficult route, but it was the only way to go if he was to receive eternal life.

The only way to receive eternal life is through Jesus Christ.

The Christian life is hard, as it was for Christian in *The Pilgrim's Progress*. There are many mistakes that we will make and problems that we will face. Charles Spurgeon knew this. He didn't have an easy life. There were many difficulties facing him.

For all those who believe in Jesus Christ, there are going to be difficulties and troubles, but it is more than worth it in the end.

'Life! Life! Eternal Life!' was what Christian longed for in *The Pilgrim's Progress*.

Make sure you obtain it through Jesus Christ.

'For the wages of sin is death; but the gift of God is eternal life through Jesus Christ our Lord.'
(Romans 6:23)

5. Oh, Susannah!

Spurgeon asked Susannah if she was praying for the one who would be her husband. From that moment, she began to pray for Charles.

Marriage is an important decision and something to pray about, even if you are still too young to wed.

Pray that the Lord will lead you towards his will for your life – whether that be a life of marriage or singleness.

Pray that your choice of husband or wife will be God's choice for you. Pray that God will choose a husband or wife for you who honours and loves Him. That is the most important thing in choosing a potential mate.

Pray that God will rule the affections of your heart, that you will love God first and foremost, and that if you fall in love with someone, it will be with one who loves Jesus most of all.

'Thou shalt love the Lord thy God with all thy heart, and with all thy soul, and with all thy strength, and with all thy mind; and thy neighbour as thyself.'
(Luke 10:27)

6. A Broken Balcony

Don't let the devil win the war within you. The Bible tells us to resist the devil and he will flee from you. The devil can attack us in many ways. He can tempt us to sin and he can tempt us to despair. Spurgeon suffered from depression. The dreadful incident in the theatre pushed him over the edge.

Depression is an illness that many have to struggle against. Sometimes, we just can't cope with what life throws at us.

Remember that even in the darkest hours, though, God is with us.

Even though we doubt and might think he doesn't care about us, we know that isn't true. We know that God is true and what He has said is true. So we can know that, in actual fact, He is here with us, helping us. We may be too tired and exhausted to feel His strength, but still trust in Him to support you and bring you home to heaven at last.

'But you, God, see the trouble of the afflicted; you consider their grief and take it in hand. The victims commit themselves to you; you are the helper of the fatherless.'
(Psalm 10:14 NIV)

7. Father to the Orphans

Orphans: There were thousands of them on the streets of Victorian Britain. Throughout the world today, many children are left without parents through death and disease.

You can lose your parents at a young age or as an adult – and it hurts, whatever age you are.

God understands – He knows what it is like to see the death of one that He loves. His Son, Jesus Christ died on the cross.

God reaches out to those who are heartbroken, mourning and sad.

Come to him with your troubles.

He will help you.

He will comfort.

'Yea, though I walk through the valley of the shadow of death, I will fear no evil: for thou art with me, thy rod and thy staff they comfort me.'
(Psalm 23:4)

8. Memories from Mentone

Charles received lots of correspondence from people of all walks of life: friends, people he had helped, poor, rich, educated ... He also received letters from D. L. Moody the American Evangelist. Moody was referred to as 'Crazy Moody' because his compassion drove him to the poorest places.

What does your compassion drive you to do? Is it compassion and love that rule your life? When you make decisions, is it your ambition that is your driving force?

Christ's driving force was love. His compassion drove Him to the cross to die for sinners.

You would be crazy to ignore this salvation.

**'How shall we escape if we neglect
so great salvation?'
(Hebrews 2:3)**

9. Grace for Gout

Spurgeon said, 'We can do without fancy speeches and fine eloquence, but we cannot do without Christ and Christ crucified.'

This is what should be in our minds when we go to listen to a preacher or to a Sunday school teacher.

We should be looking for Jesus.

We should be searching for Him for ourselves.

We should be searching for Jesus Christ, crucified because it is in His death that we have life – eternal life.

'He that heareth my word and believeth on him that sent me, hath everlasting life and shall not come into condemnation; but is passed from death unto life.'
(John 5:24)

10. The Queen Arrives

Again, the author imagines the Queen of England coming to hear the Prince of Preachers. He tries to imagine what her thoughts would have been, were she to have listened to one of his sermons.

What are your thoughts after reading this book?

Are you content where you are?

Have you given your life to Christ?

Are you living to please Him?

Is it possible that the Queen of England was taught by the Prince of Preachers to love the King of Heaven?

We do not know.

But you have to ask that question about yourself.

Has finding out about Spurgeon's life and his Lord Jesus, brought you to understand that you need to be saved from your sins?

**'When I was brought low, he saved me.'
(Psalm 116:6 NIV)**

Spurgeon books available from Christian Focus Publications

According To Promise
All of Grace
Around the Wicket Gate
Chequebook Of The Bank Of Faith
Christ's Glorious Achievements
Come Ye Children
Complete John Ploughman (The)
Counsel for Christian Workers
Faith
Greatest Fight in the World (The)
John Ploughman's Talks
Lectures to My Students
Mother, Sister and Follower
No Tears in Heaven
Only A Prayer Meeting
Queen Victoria's Request
Saint And His Saviour (The)
Soul Winner (The)
Morning and Evening
Most Holy Place (The)
Spurgeon Prayers
Till He Come

For a full list of Trailblazers, please see our website: www.christianfocus.com
All Trailblazers are available as e-books

Christian Focus Publications publishes books for adults and children under its four main imprints: Christian Focus, CF4K, Mentor and Christian Heritage. Our books reflect our conviction that God's Word is reliable and Jesus is the way to know him, and live for ever with him.

Our children's publication list covers pre-school to early teens. We also publish personal and family devotional titles, biographies and inspirational stories that children will love.

From pre-school board books to teenage apologetics, we have it covered!

Find us at our web page:
www.christianfocus.com